Masterpieces of Tintoretto (1908)

ISBN-13 : 978-1512312249
ISBN-10 : 151231224X

Notice

This documentary study use historic, archived documents. Because of this, some pages may look blurry or low quality. Still are included in this book because they have high value from critical, documentary, historical, informative and journalistic point of view .

Dtp
and
visual art

Iacob Adrian

THE
MASTERPIECES
OF
TINTORETTO
(1518-1594)

Sixty reproductions of photographs from the original paintings, affording examples of the different characteristics of the Artist's work

Author statement

This is a series of art books .

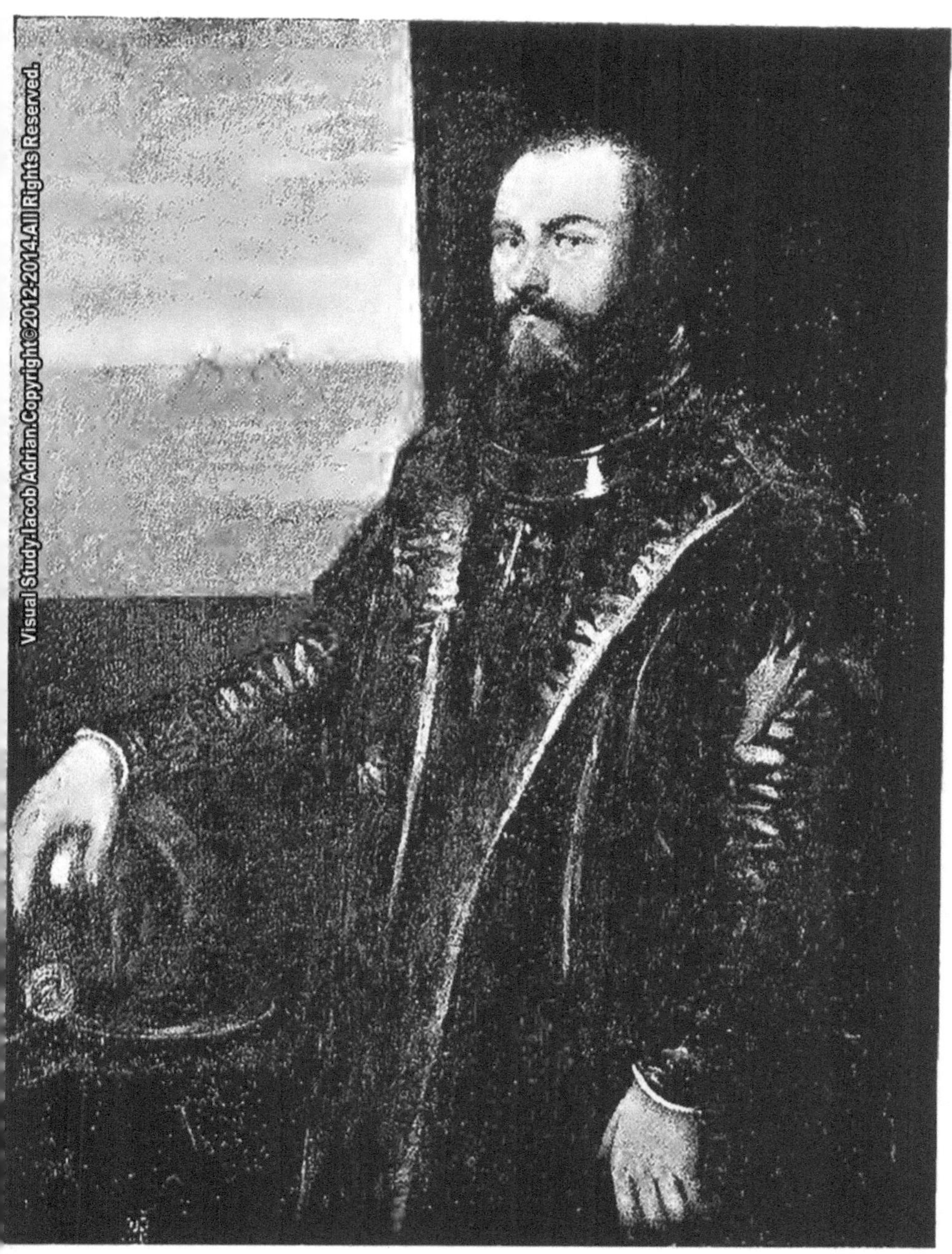

ADMIRAL VENIERO
(*Uffizi, Florence*)

L'AMIRAL VENIERO
(*Galerie des Offices, Florence*)

ADMIRAL VENIERO
(*Florenz, Uffizien*)
Frat. Alinari, Photo.

This little Book conveys the greetings of

....

to

....

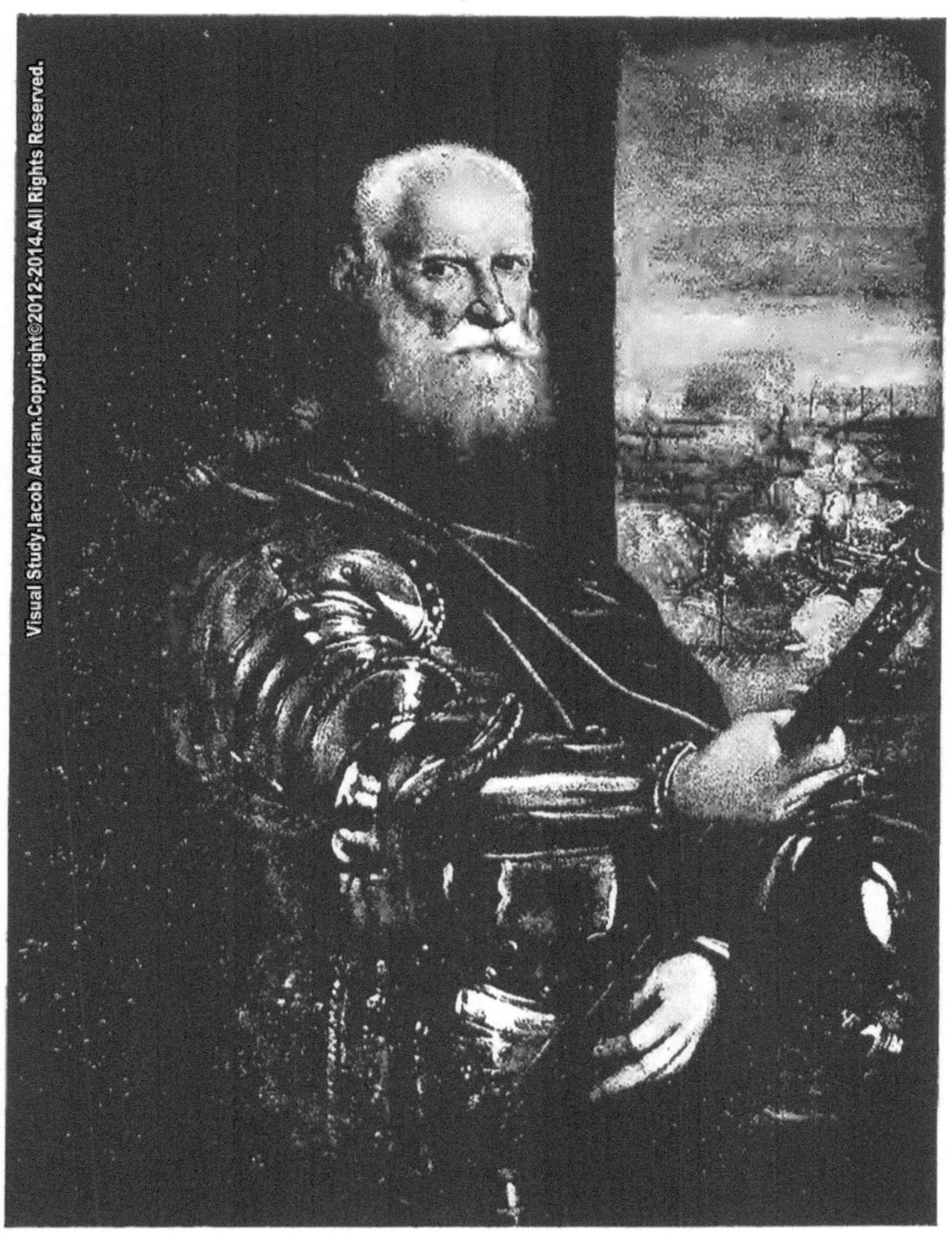

ADMIRAL VENIERO
(*Imperial Gallery, Vienna*)

L'AMIRAL VENIERO
(*Galerie impériale, Vienne*)

ADMIRAL VENIERO
(*Wien, Kaiserl. Galerie*)

F. Hanfstaengl, Photo.

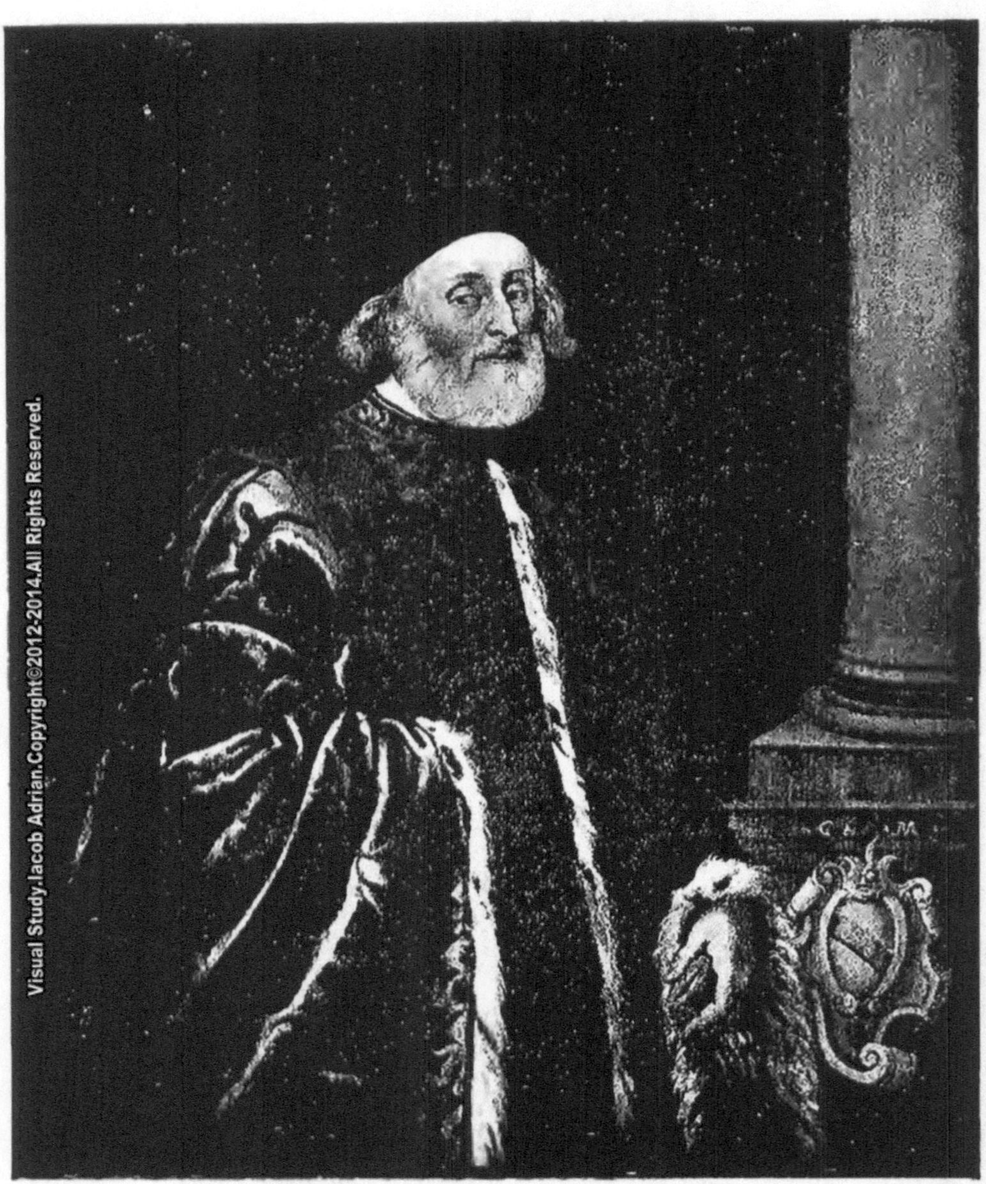

Carlo Morosini
(*Academy, Venice*)

Carlo Morosini
(*Académie, Venise*)

Carlo Morosini
(*Venedig, Akademie*)
D. Anderson, Photo.

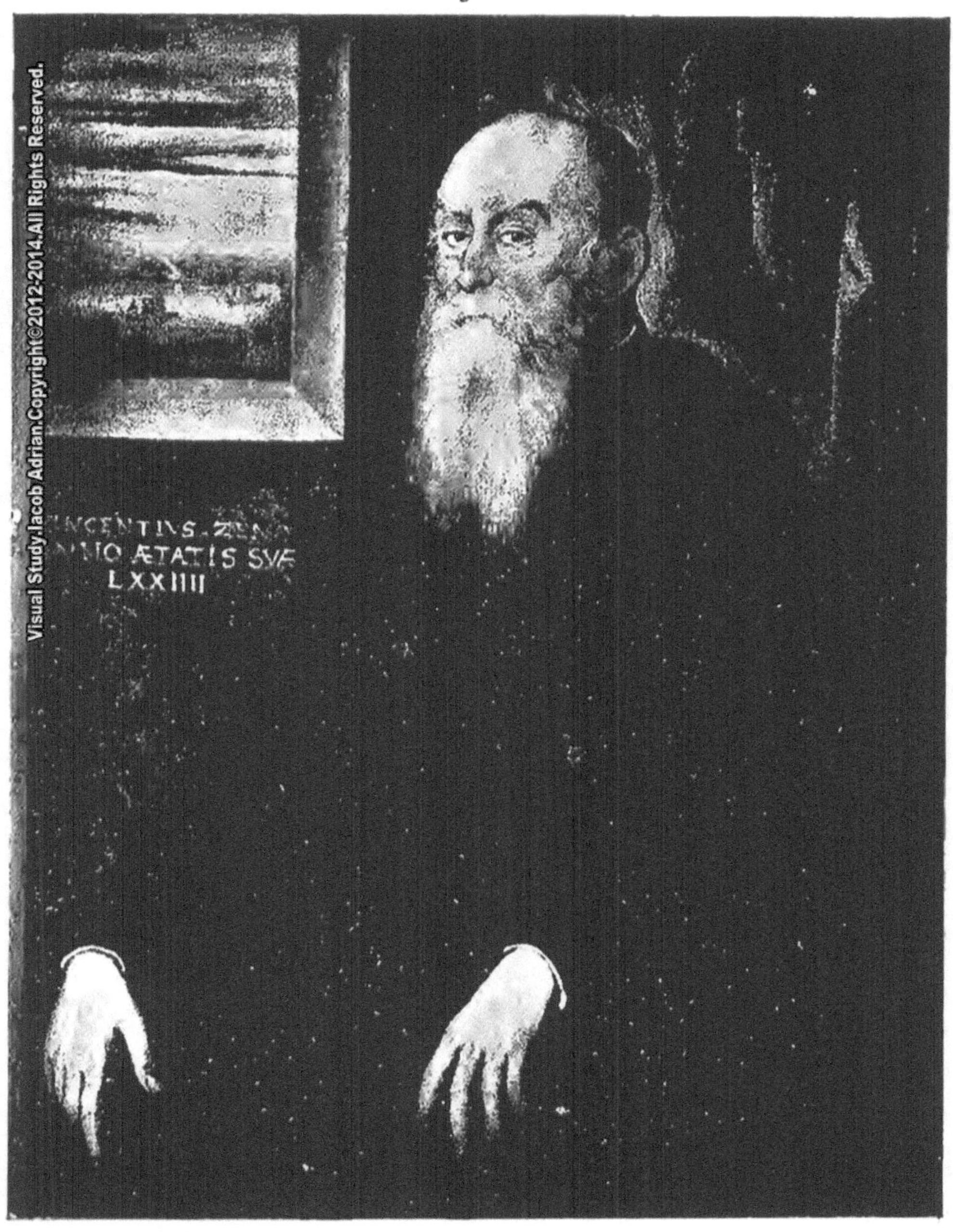

VINCENZO ZENO
(*Pitti, Florence*)

VINCENZO ZENO
(*Galerie Pitti, Florence*)

VINCENZO ZENO
(*Florenz, Galerie Pitti*)
D. Anderson, Photo.

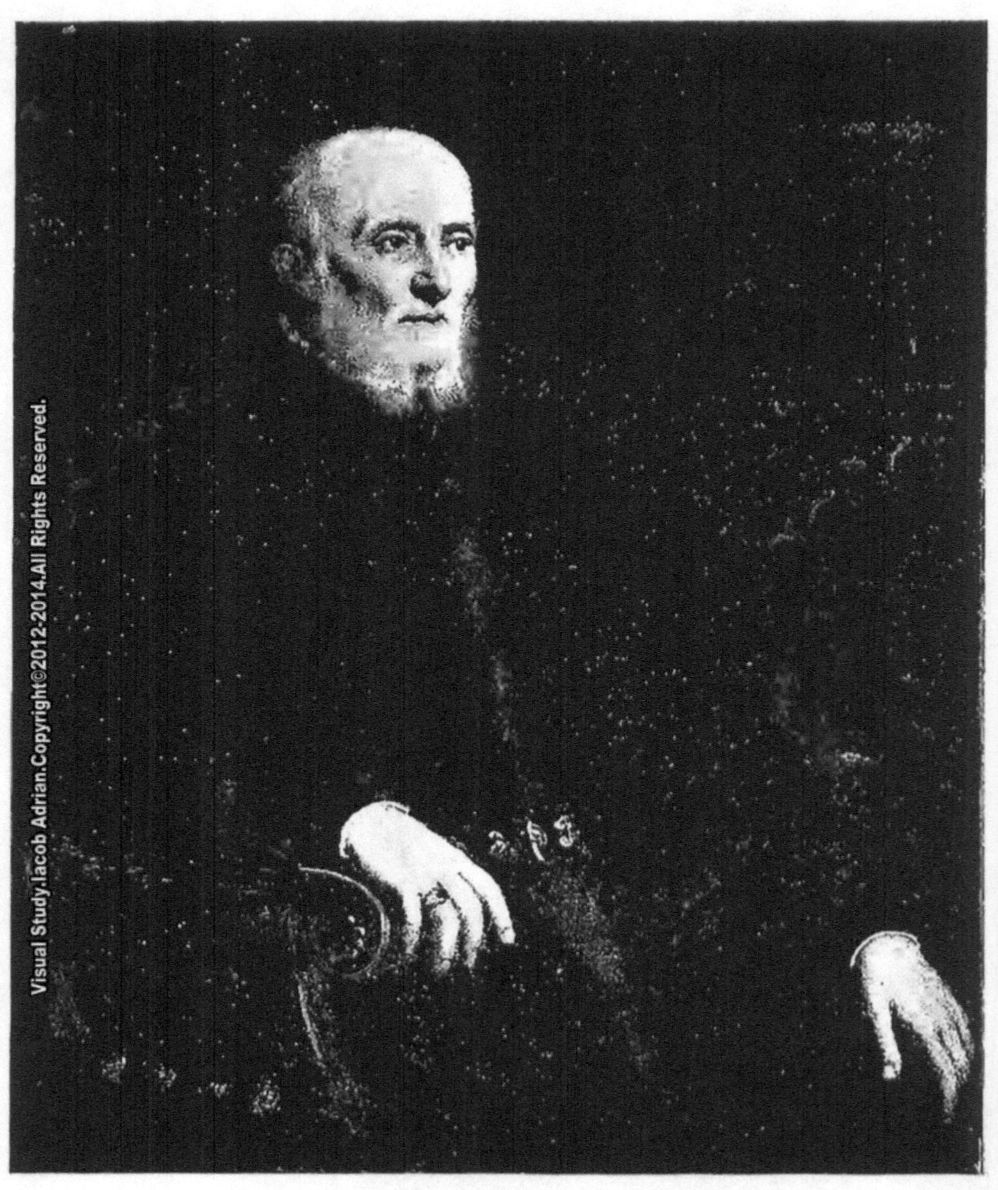

LUIGI CORNARO
(*Pitti, Florence*)

LUIGI CORNARO
(*Galerie Pitti, Florence*)

LUIGI CORNARO
(*Florenz, Galerie Pitti*)
D. Anderson, Photo.

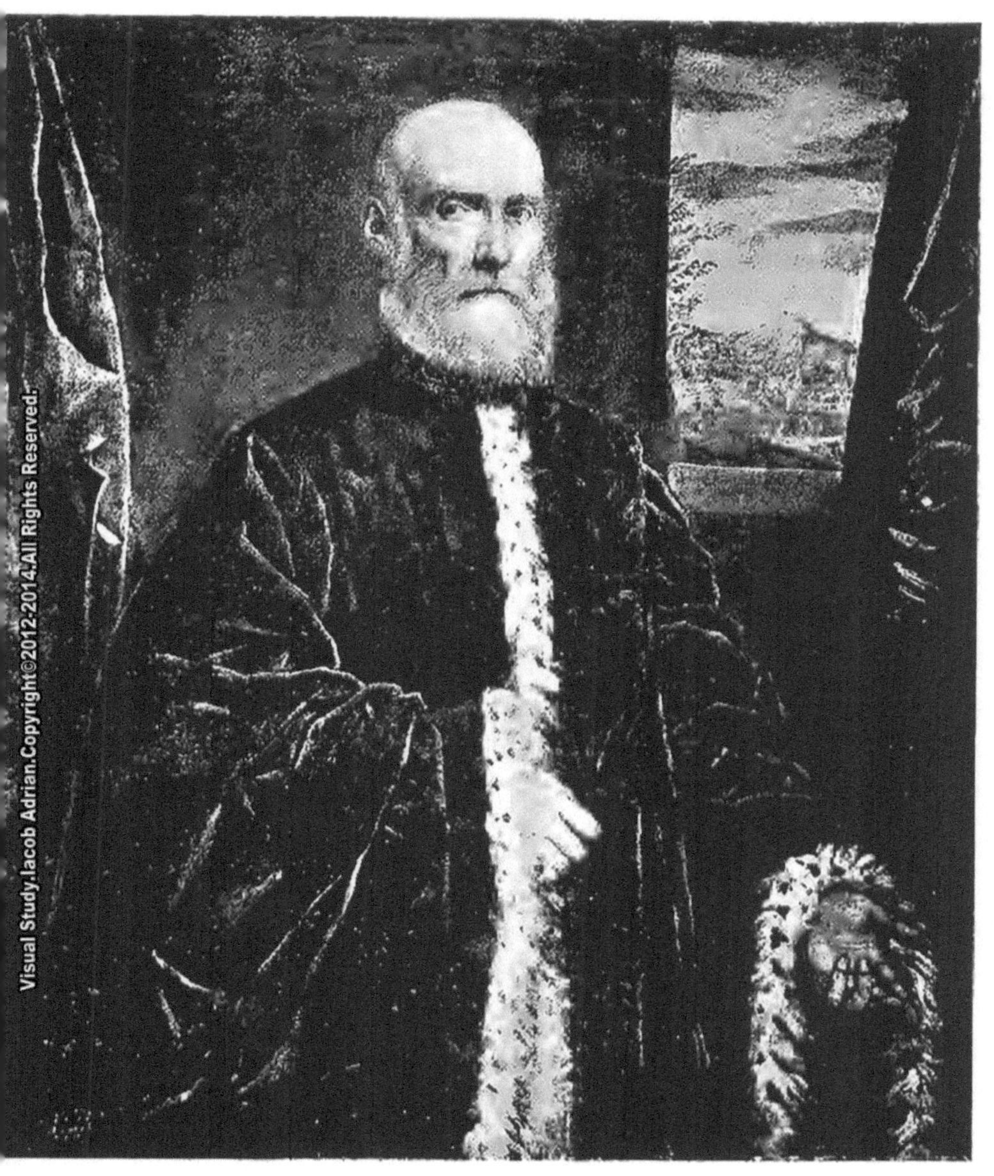

PORTRAIT OF A PROCURATOR
(*Royal Gallery, Berlin*)

PORTRAIT D'UN PROCURATEUR
(*Galerie royale, Berlin*)

BILDNIS EINES PROKURATORS
(*Berlin, Kgl. Galerie*)

F. Hanfstaengl, Photo.

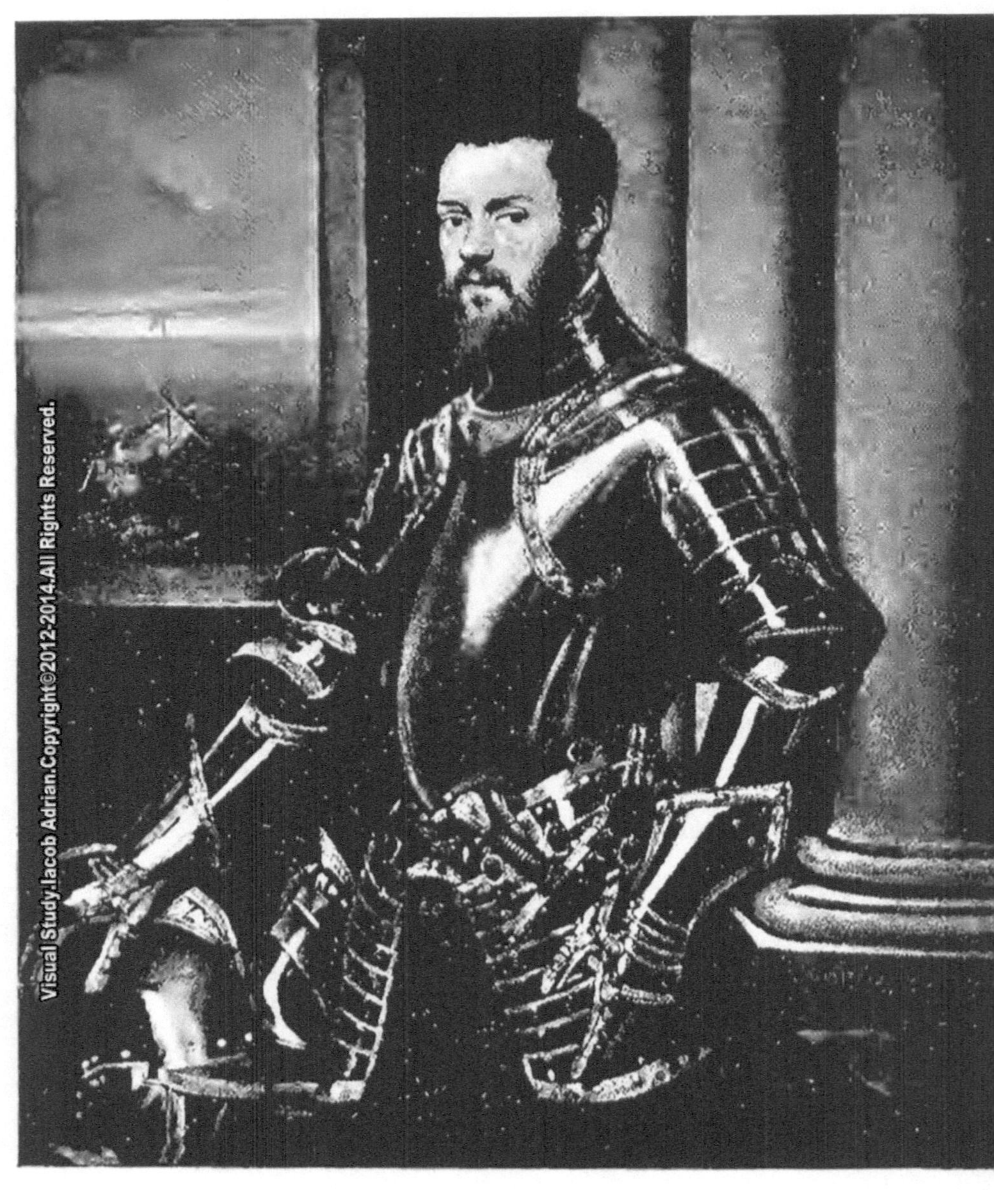

A Man in Armour
(*Imperial Gallery, Vienna*)

Un Homme en Armure
(*Galerie impériale, Vienne*)

Ein Mann in Rüstung
(*Wien, Kaiserl. Galerie*)

F. Hanfstaengl, Photo.

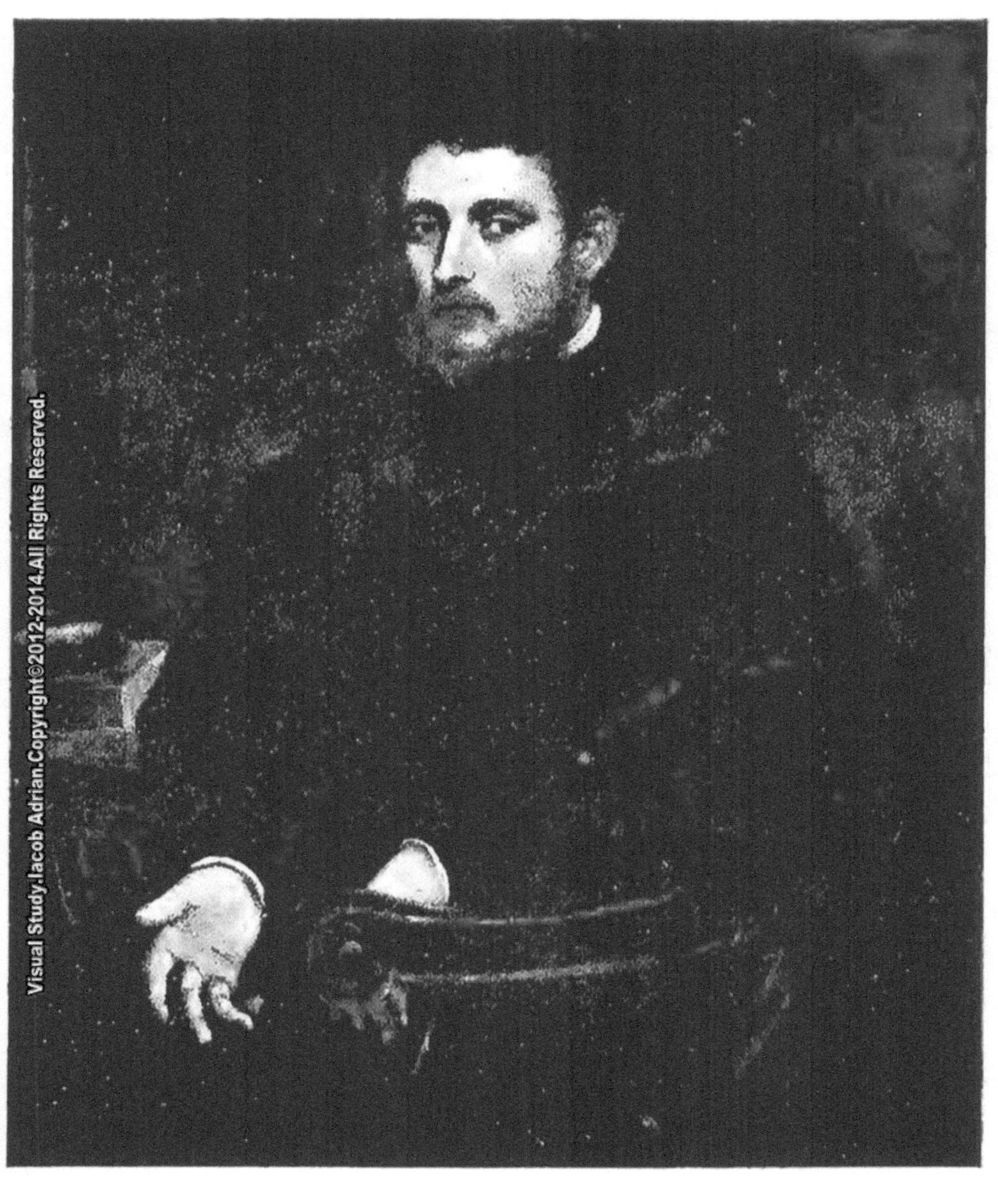

Portrait of a Man
(*Imperial Gallery, Vienna*)

Portrait d'Homme
(*Galerie impériale, Vienne*)

Bildnis eines Mannes
(*Wien, Kaiserl. Galerie*)

F. Hanfstaengl, Photo.

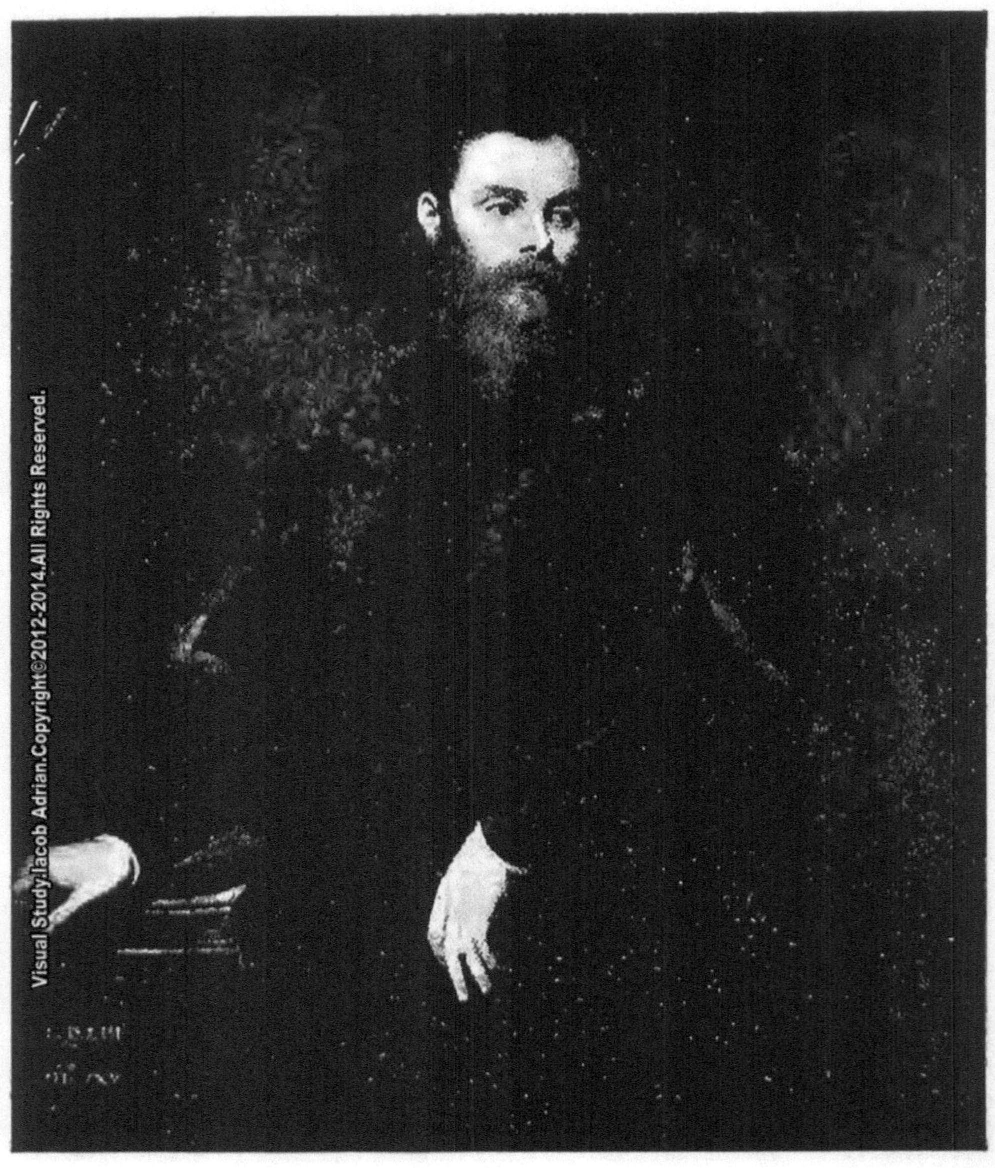

Portrait of a Man
(*Imperial Gallery, Vienna*)

Portrait d'Homme
(*Galerie impériale, Vienne*)

Bildnis eines Mannes
(*Wien, Kaiserl. Galerie*)

F. Hanfstaengl, Photo.

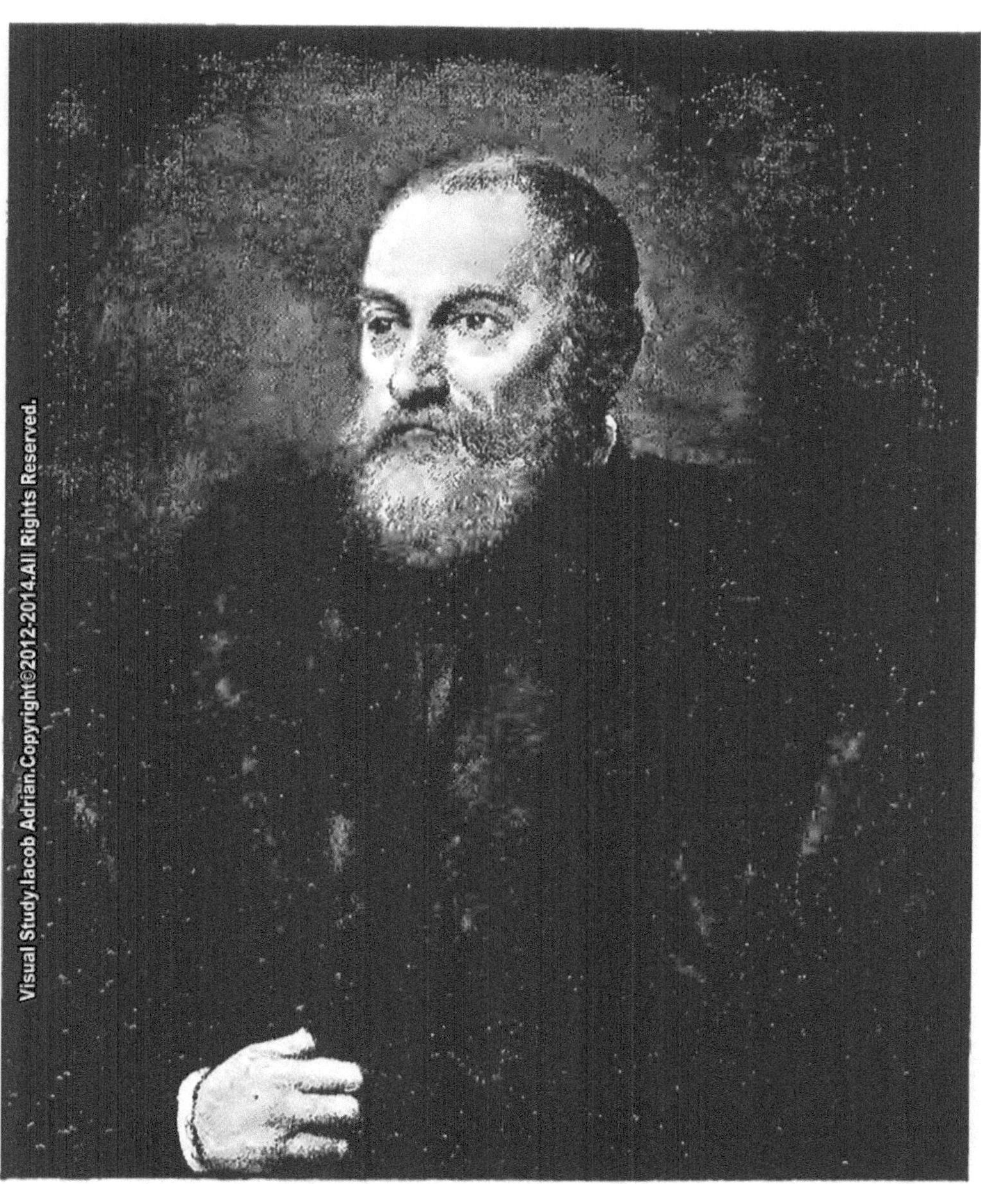

PORTRAIT OF A MAN
(*Museum, Buda-Pesth*)

PORTRAIT D'HOMME
(*Musée, Buda-Pesth*)

BILDNIS EINES MANNES
(*Budapest, Museum*)

F. Hanfstaengl, Photo.

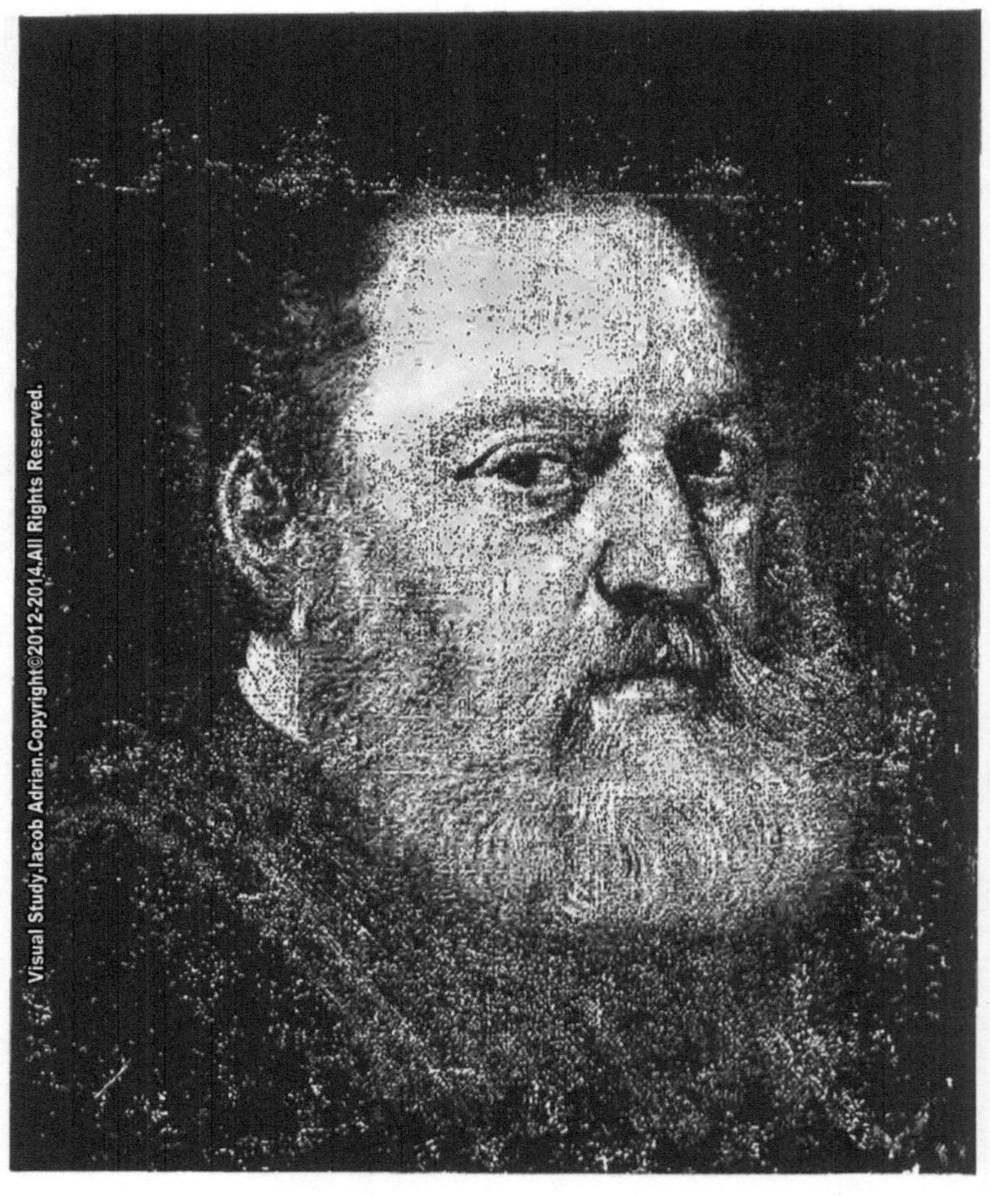

PORTRAIT OF A MAN
(*Louvre, Paris*)

PORTRAIT D'HOMME
(*Louvre, Paris*)

BILDNIS EINES MANNES
(*Paris, Louvre*)

Neurdein Frères, Photo.

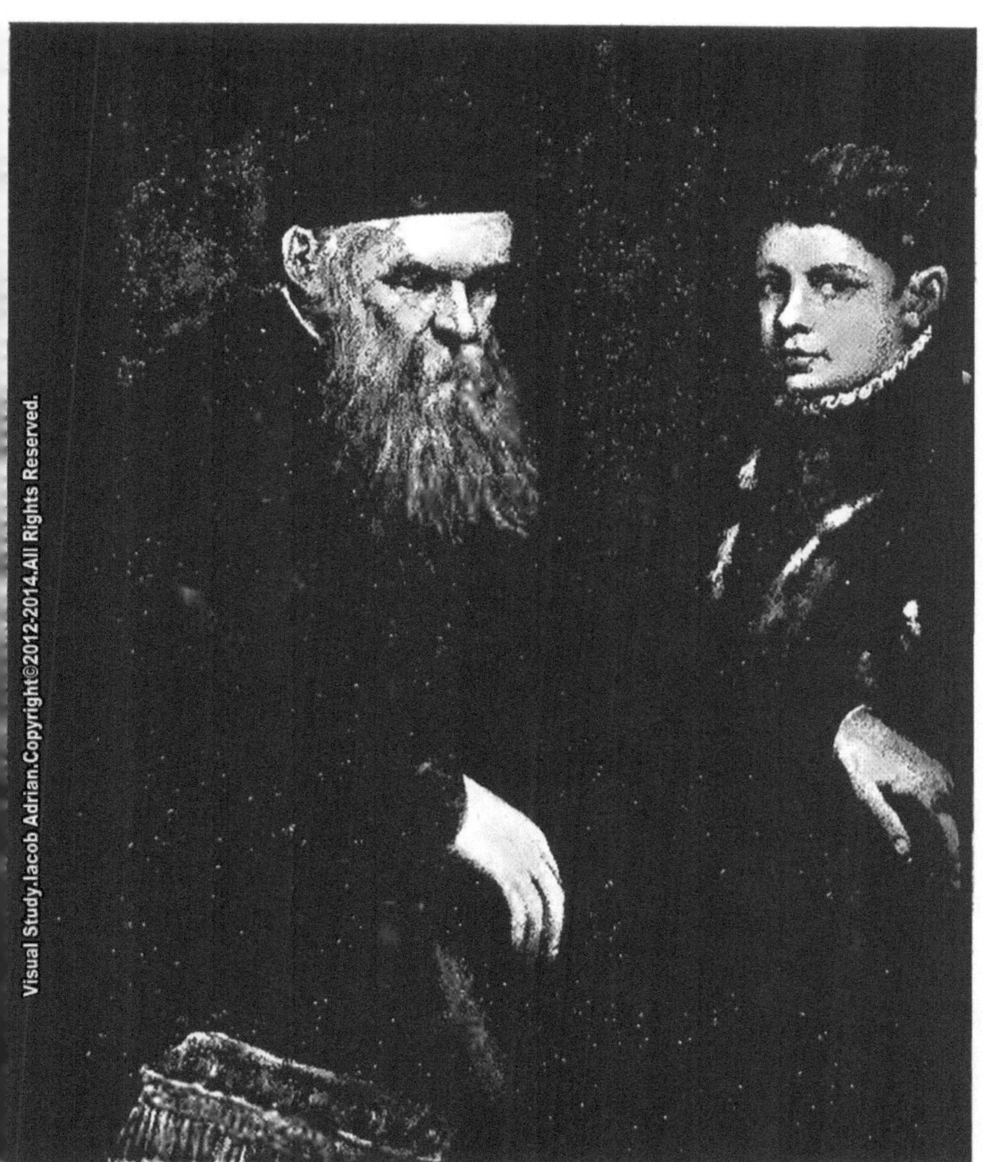

AN OLD MAN AND A BOY (*Imperial Gallery, Vienna*)

UN VIEILLARD ET UN GARÇON (*Galerie impériale, Vienne*)

EIN ALTER MANN UND EIN KNABE (*Wien, Kaiserl. Galerie*)

F. Hanfstaengl, Photo.

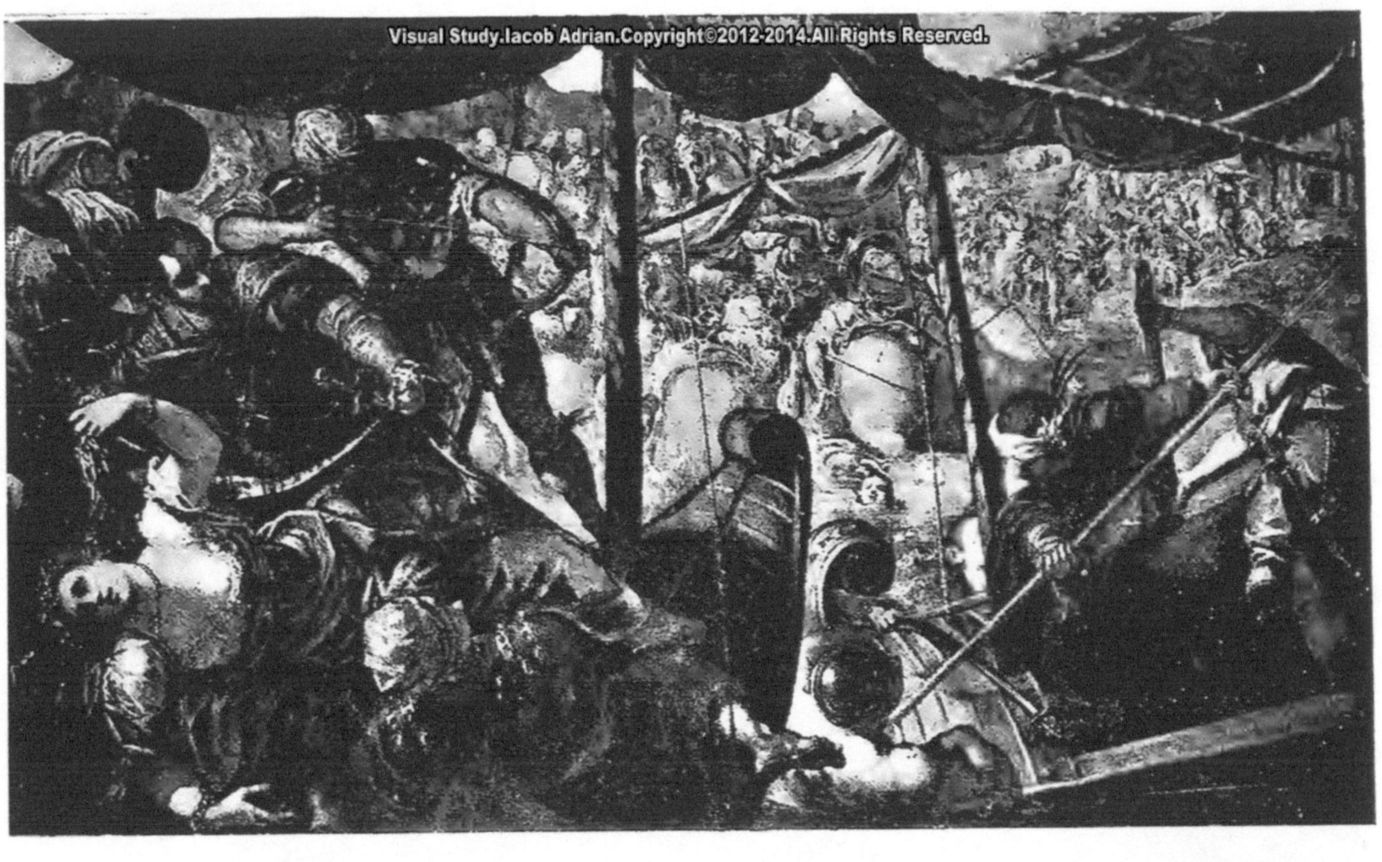

A Battle by Land and Sea
(*Prado, Madrid*)

Une Bataille sur Terre et sur Mer
(*Prado, Madrid*)

Eine Schlacht zu Wasser und zu Lande
(*Madrid, Prado*)

F. Hanfstaengl, Photo.

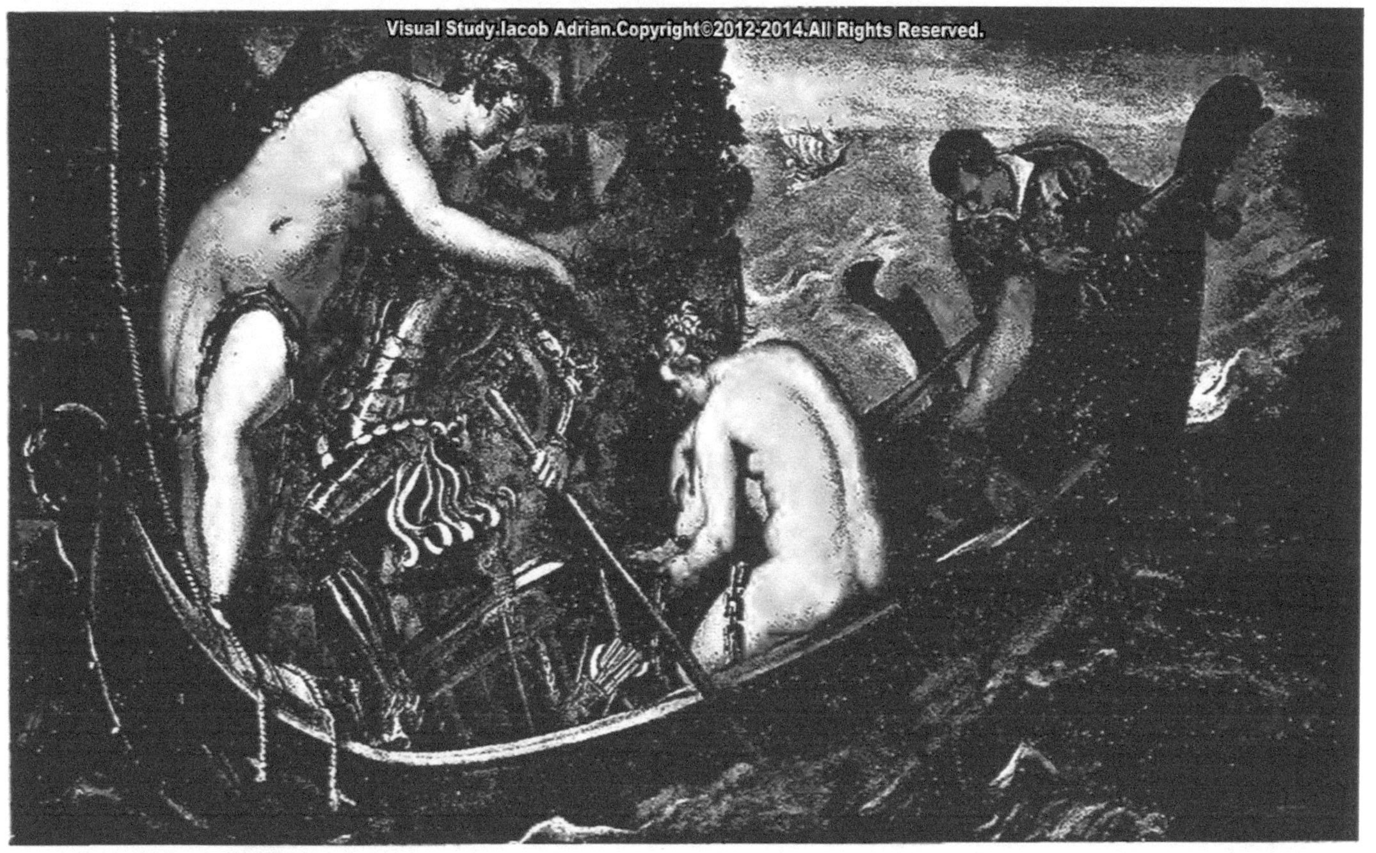

THE RESCUE
(Royal Gallery, Dresden)

DIE RETTUNG
(Dresden, Kgl. Galerie)
F. Hanfstaengl, Photo.

LA DÉLIVRANCE
(Galerie royale, Dresde)

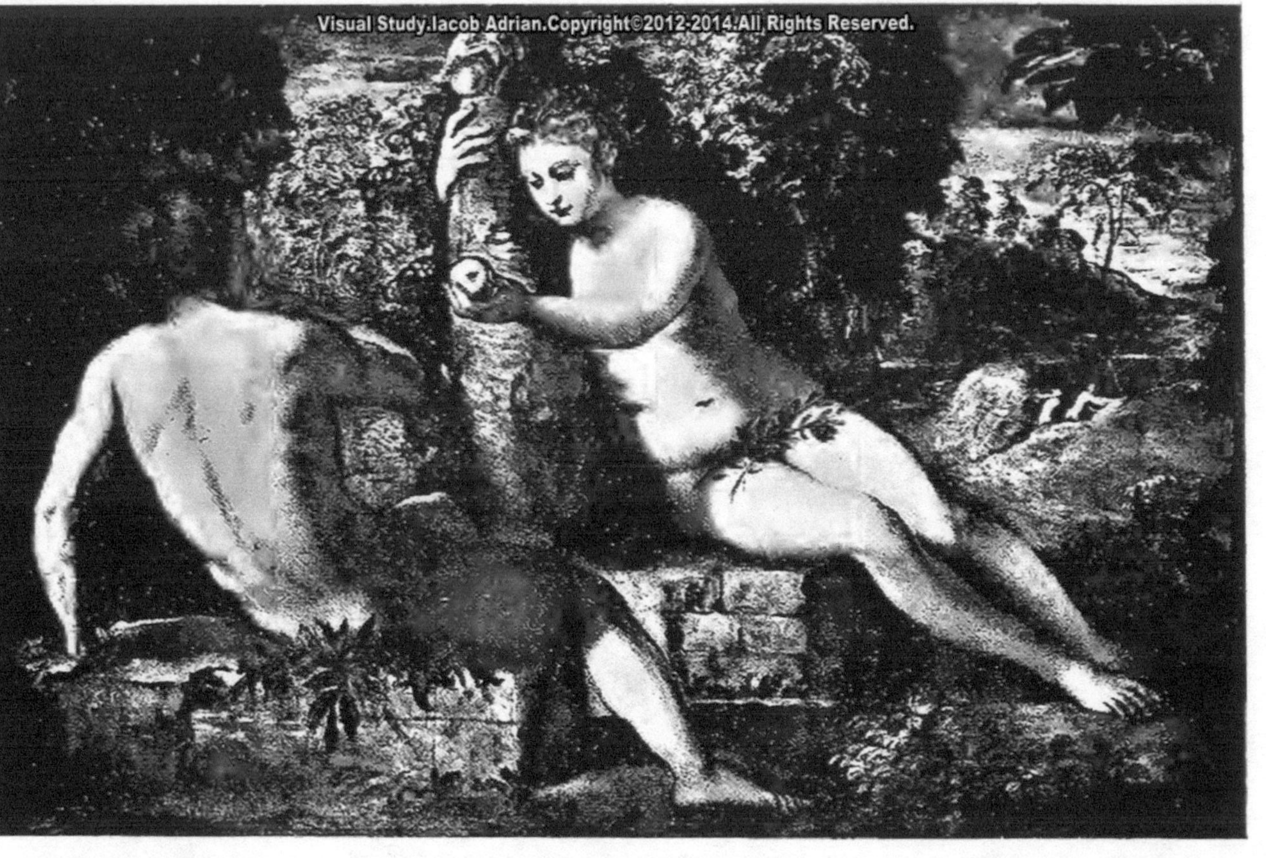

Adam and Eve
(*Academy, Venice*)

Adam und Eva
(*Venedig, Akademie*)
F. Hanfstaengl, Photo.

Adam et Ève
(*Académie, Venise*)

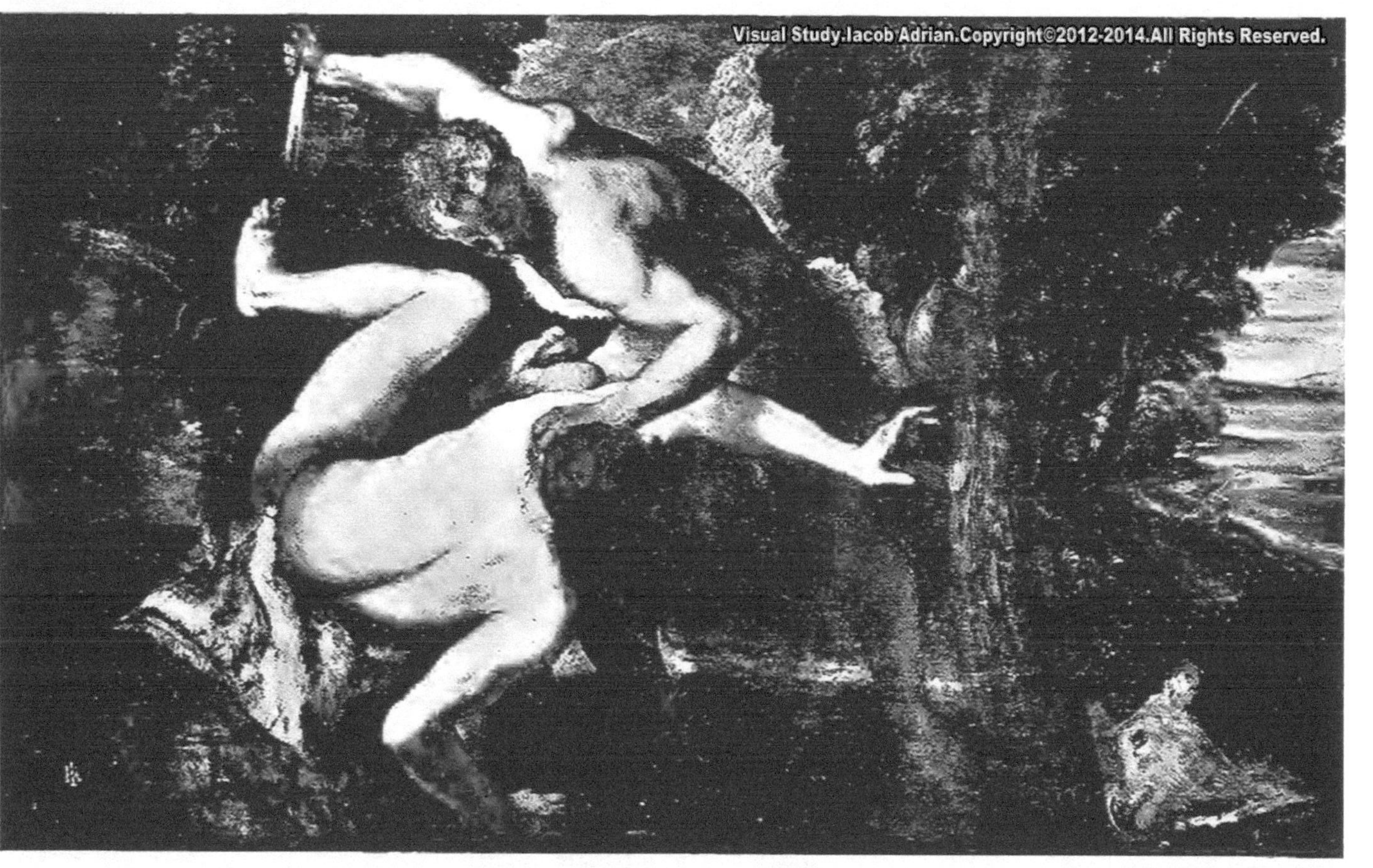

Cain and Abel
(Academy, Venice)

Kain und Abel
(Venedig, Akademie)
D. Anderson, Photo.

Caïn et Abel
(Académie, Venise)

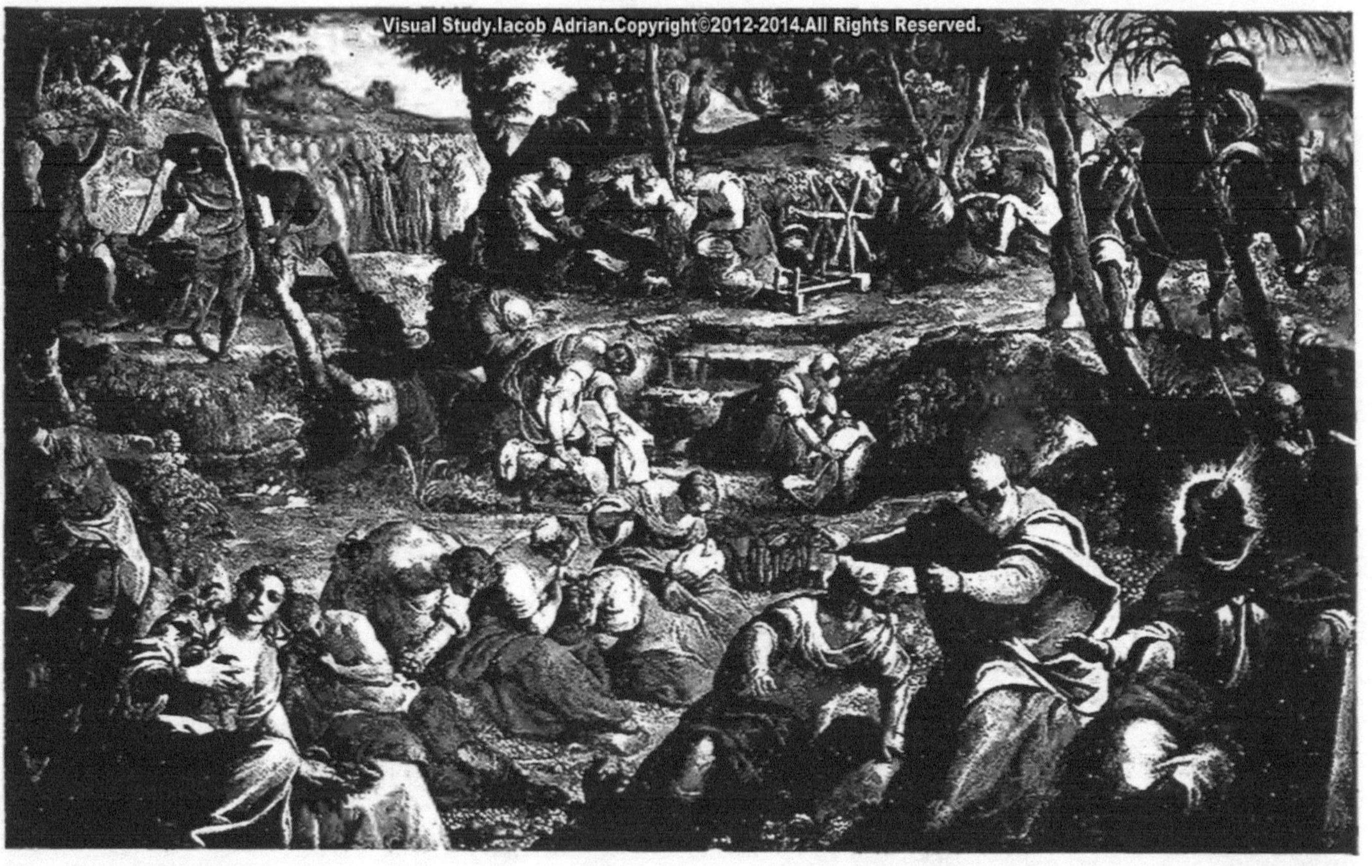

The Manna in the Desert
(*S. Giorgio Maggiore, Venice*)

Die Manna in der Wüste
(*Venedig, S. Giorgio Maggiore*)

La Manne dans le Désert
(*S. Giorgio Maggiore, Venise*)

D. Anderson, Photo.

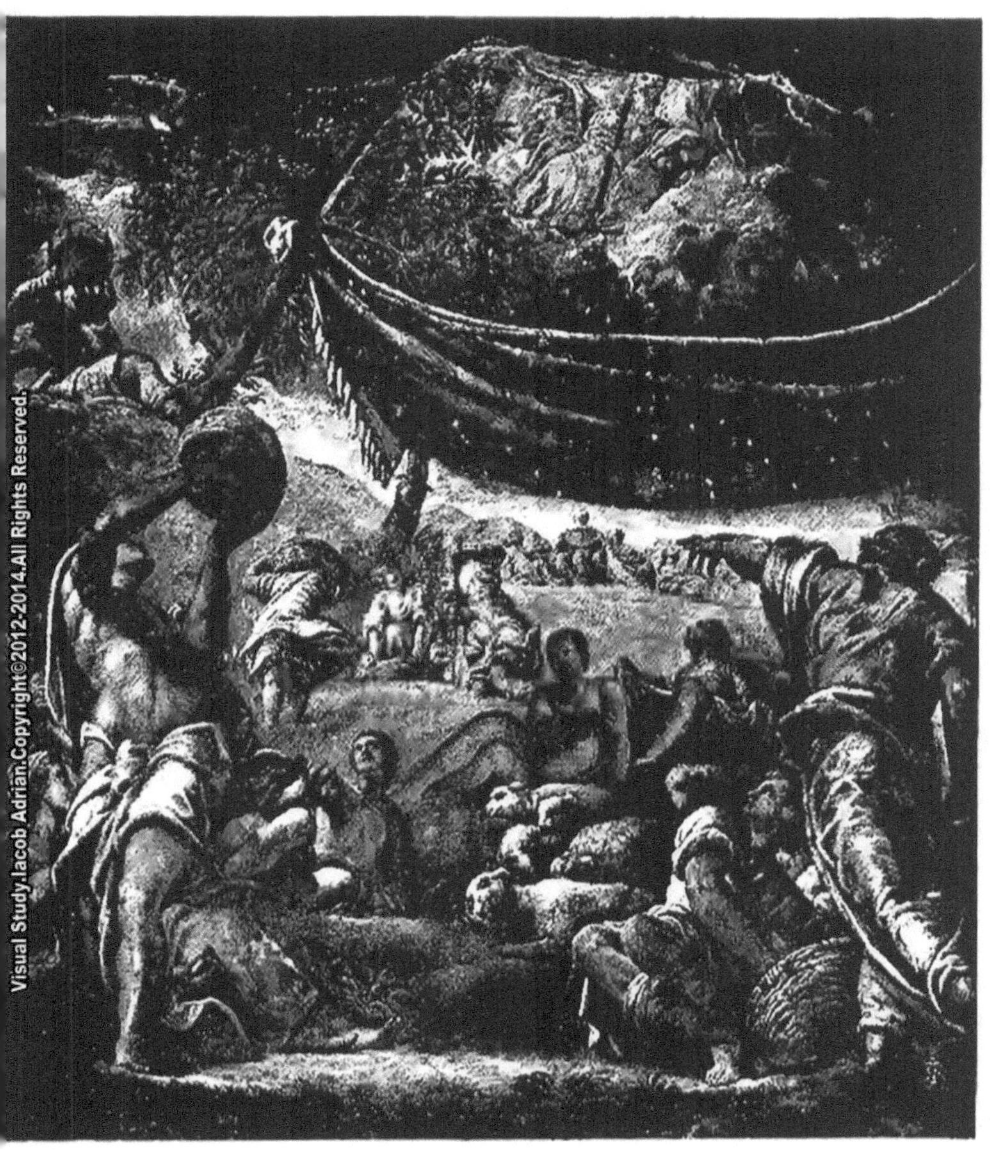

THE MANNA IN THE DESERT
(*St. Roche's, Venice*)

LA MANNE DANS LE DÉSERT
(*Église St-Roch, Venise*)

DIE MANNA IN DER WÜSTE
(*Venedig, Rochuskirche*)

D. Anderson, Photo.

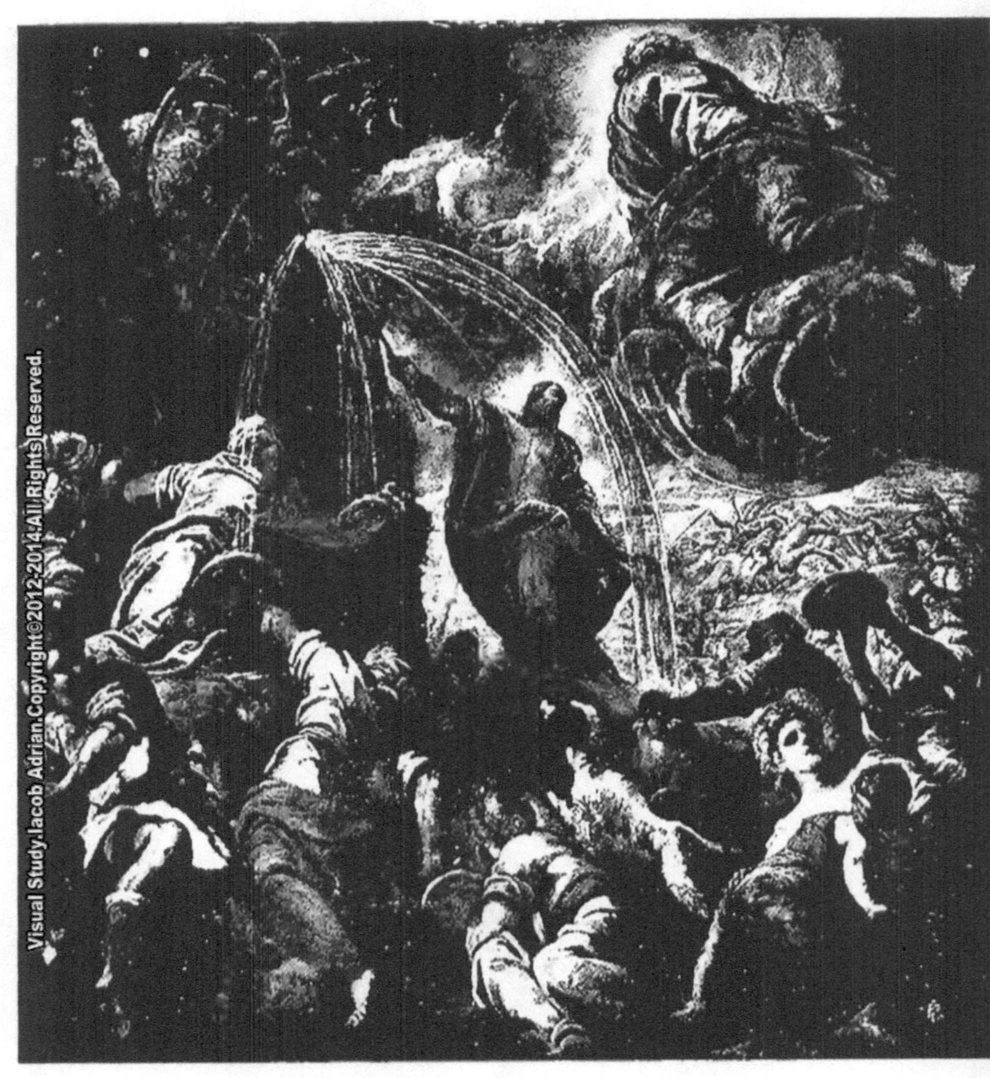

MOSES STRIKING THE ROCK
(*St. Roche's, Venice*)

MOÏSE FRAPPANT LE ROCHER
(*Église St-Roch, Venise*)

MOSES DEN FELSEN SCHLAGEND
(*Venedig, Rochuskirche*)

D. Anderson, Photo.

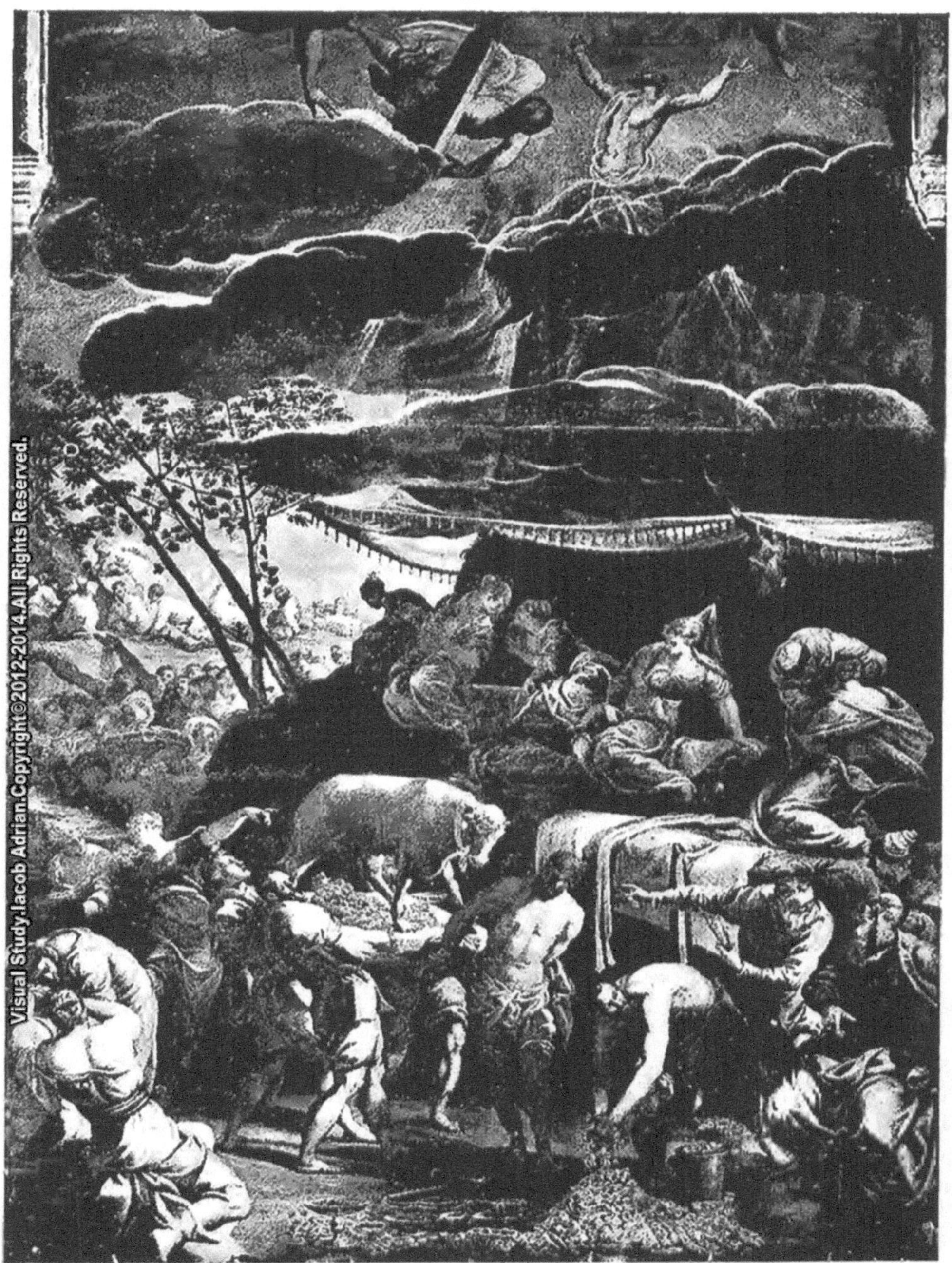

The Worship of the Golden Calf (*S. Maria dell' Orto, Venice*)

L'Adoration du Veau d'Or (*S. Maria dell' Orto, Venise*)

Die Anbetung des goldenen Kalbes (*Venedig, S. Maria dell' Orto*) *D. Anderson, Photo.*

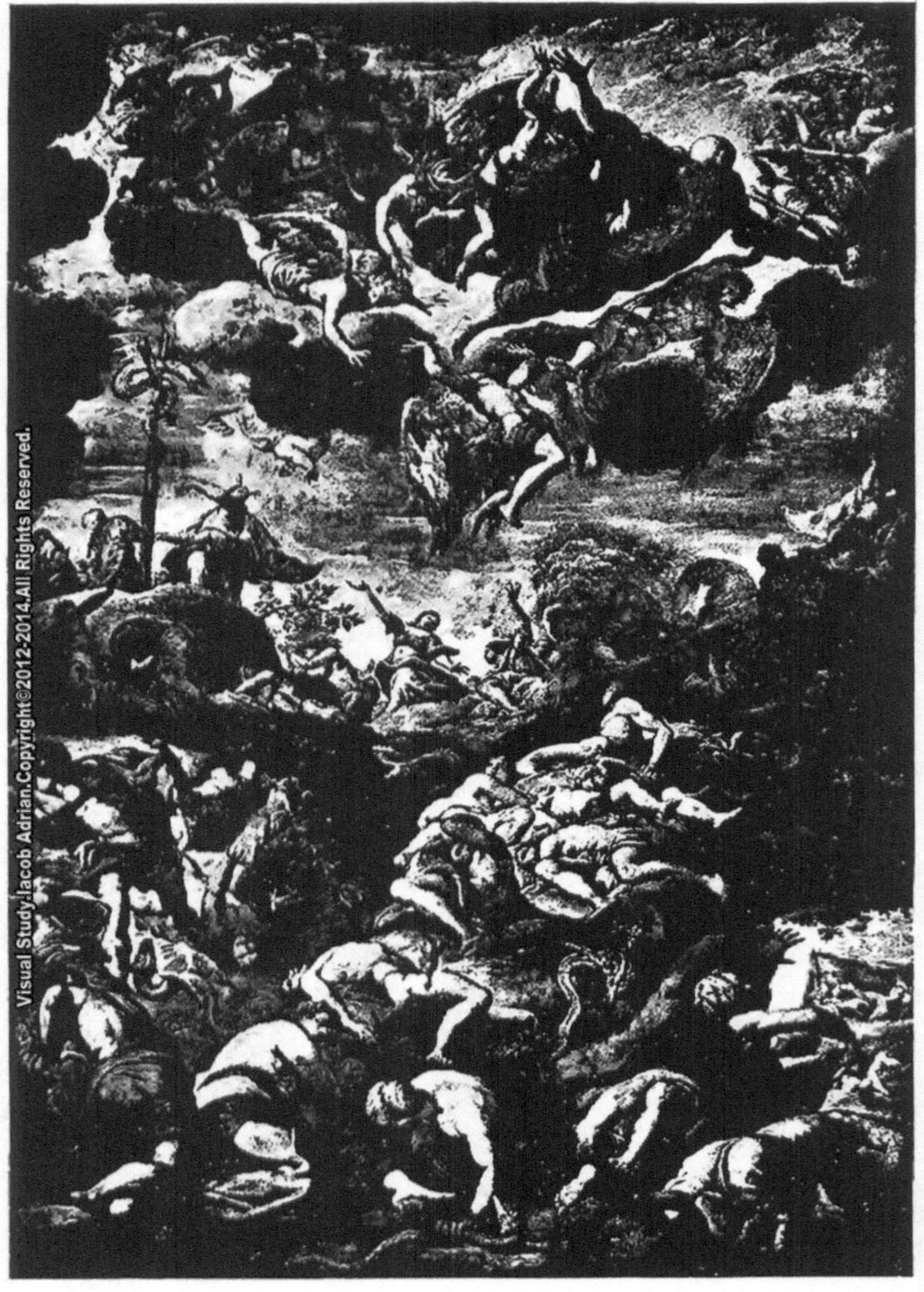

THE PLAGUE OF SERPENTS (*St. Roche's, Venice*)

LA PLAIE DES SERPENTS (*Église St-Roch, Venise*)

DIE PLAGE VON SCHLANGEN (*Venedig, Rochuskirche*)

D. Anderson, Photo.

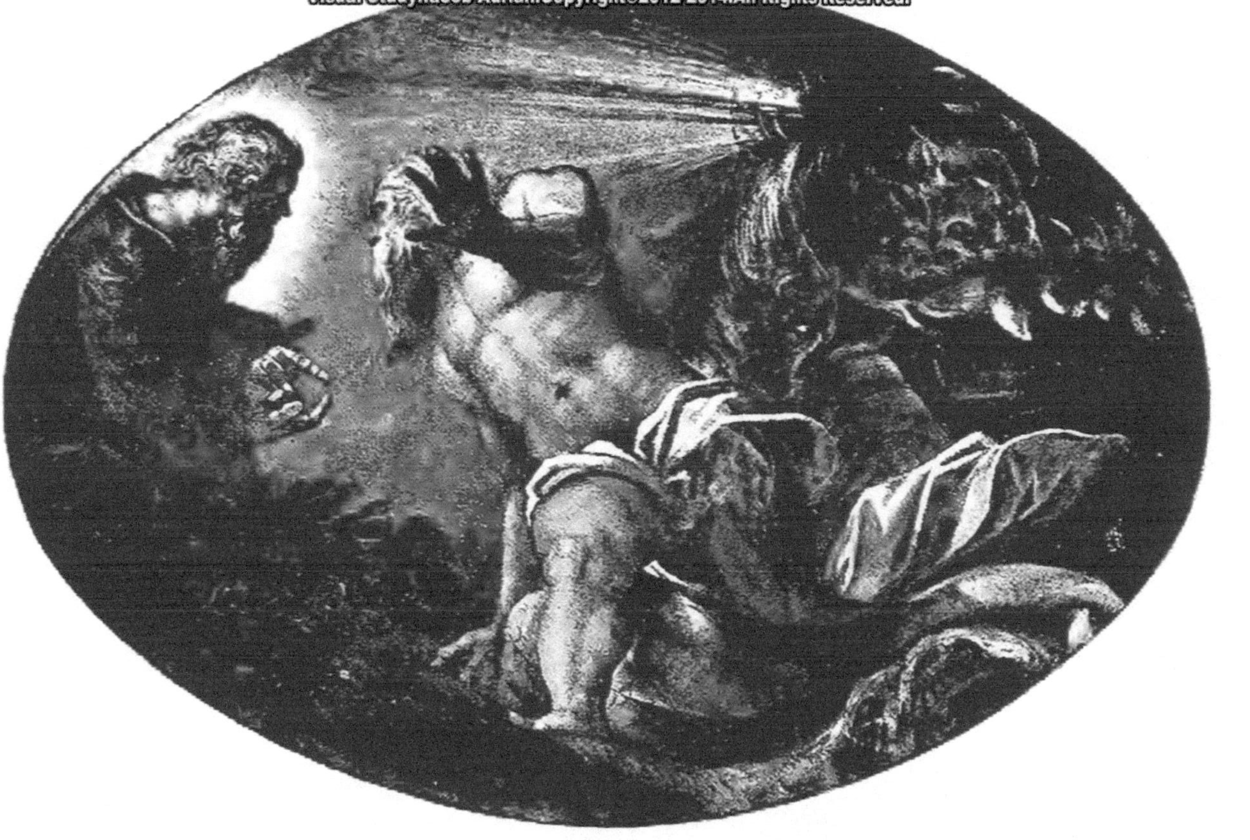

JONAH
St. Roche's, Venice)

JONA
(Venedig, Rochuskirche)
D. Anderson, Photo.

JONAS
(Église St-Roch, Venise)

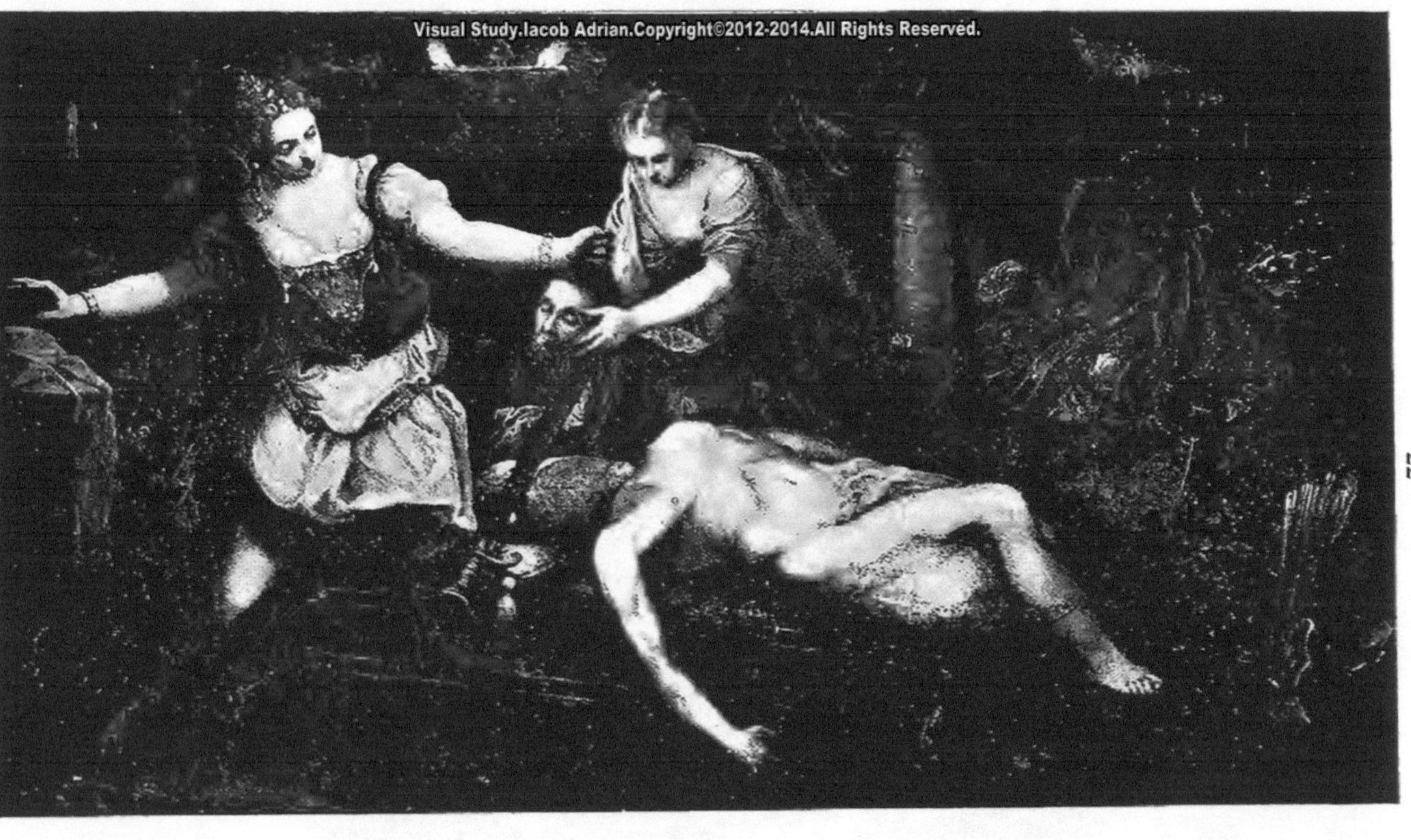

Judith and Holophernes
(*Prado, Madrid*)

Judith und Holofernes
(*Madrid, Prado*)
F. Hanfstaengl, Photo.

Judith et Holopherne
(*Prado, Madrid*)

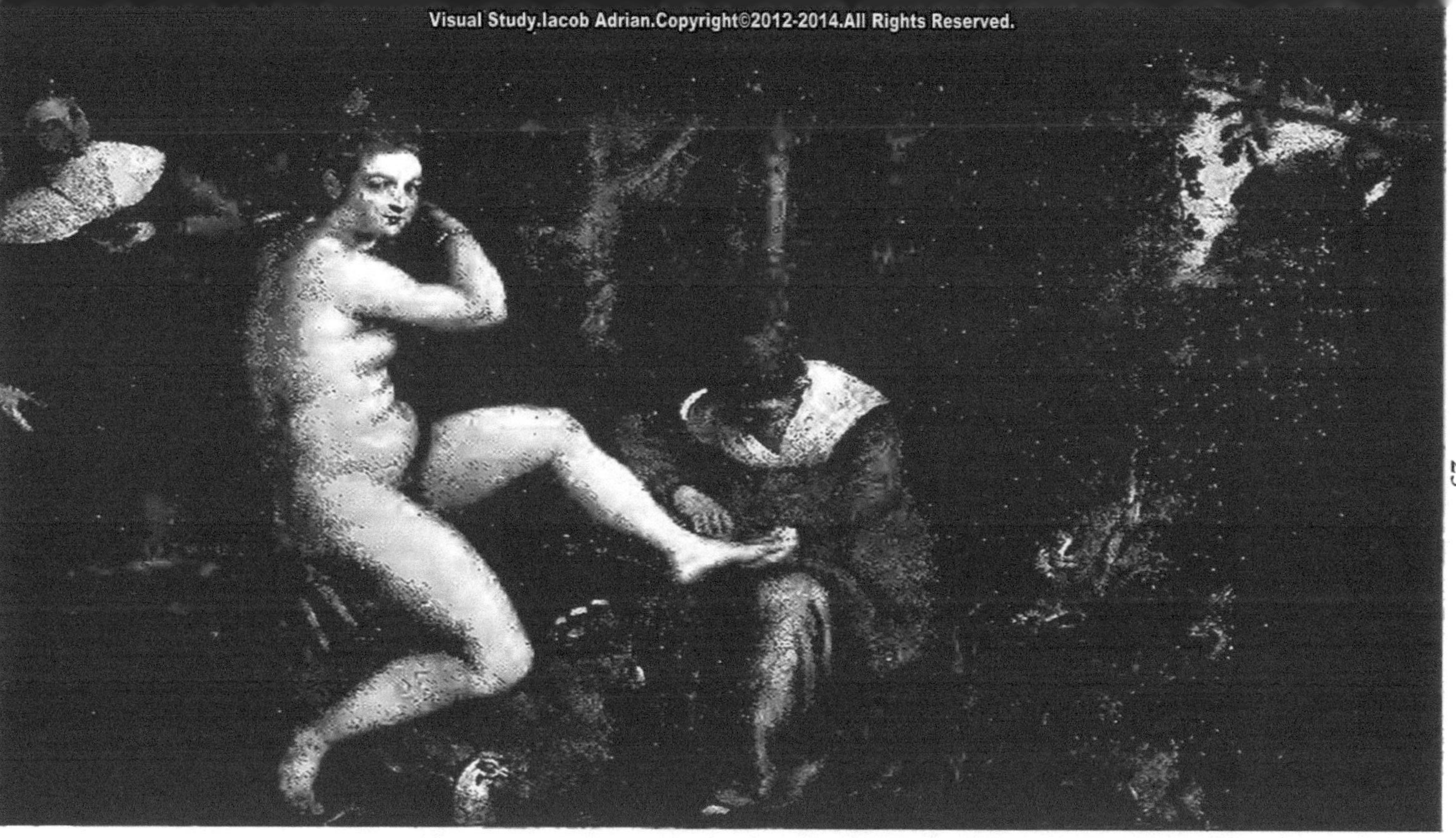

SUSANNA AND THE ELDERS
(Louvre, Paris)

SUSANNA UND DIE ALTEN
(Paris, Louvre)
F. Hanfstaengl, Photo.

SUZANNE ET LES VIEILLARDS
(Louvre, Paris)

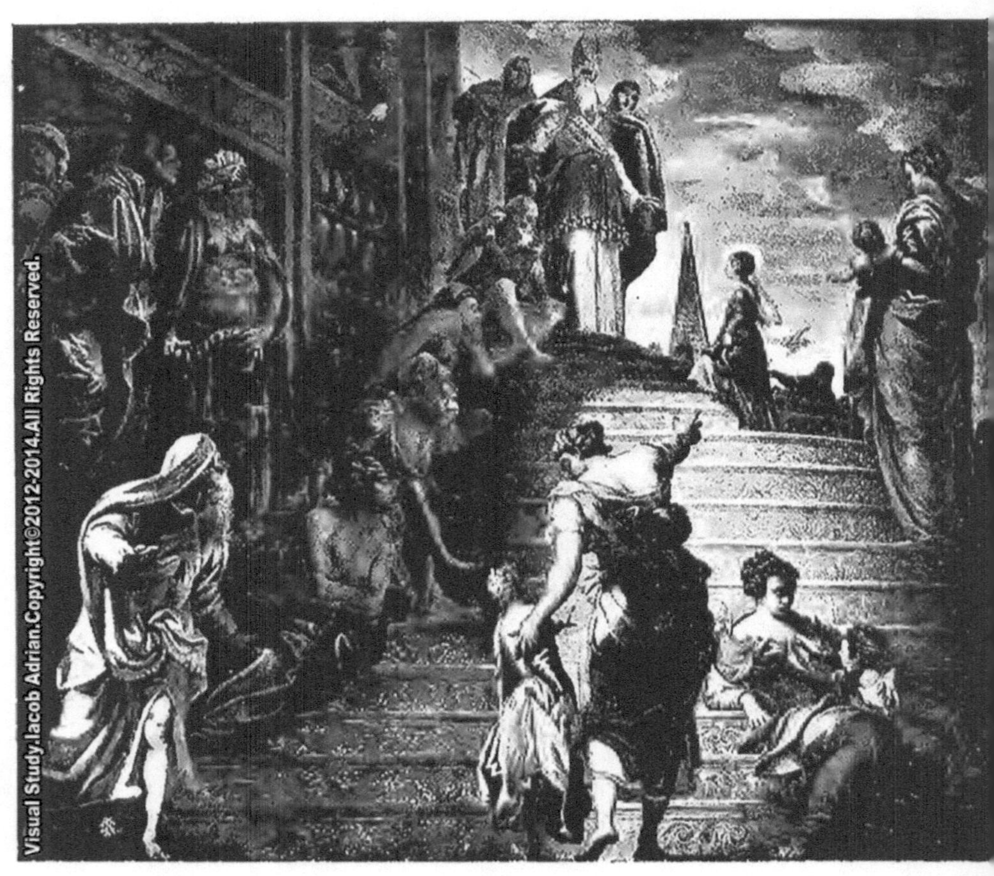

THE PRESENTATION OF THE VIRGIN
(*S. Maria dell' Orto, Venice*)

LA PRÉSENTATION DE LA VIERGE
(*S. Maria dell' Orto, Venise*)

MARIÄ OPFER
(*Venedig, S. Maria dell' Orto*)

D. Anderson, Photo.

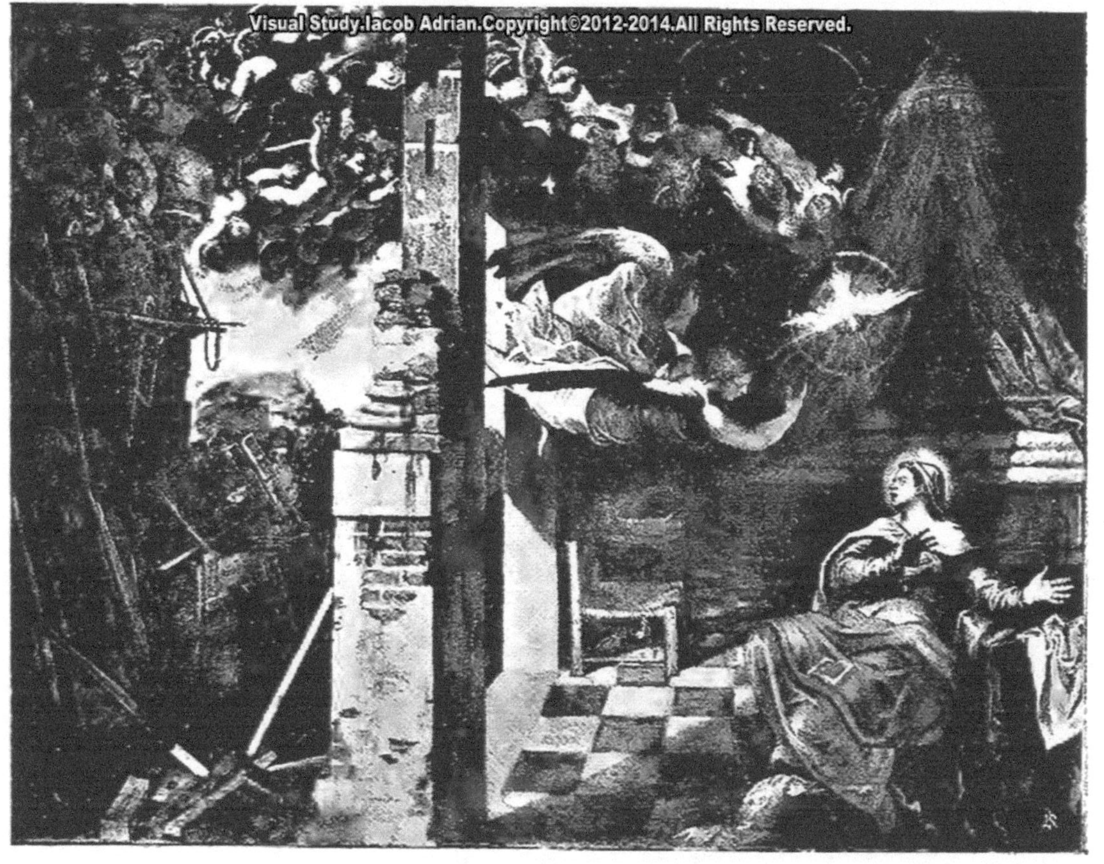

THE ANNUNCIATION
(*St. Roche's, Venice*)

MARIÄ VERKÜNDIGUNG
(*Venedig, Rochuskirche*)
D. Anderson, Pho.o.

L'ANNONCIATION
(*Église St-Roch, Venise*)

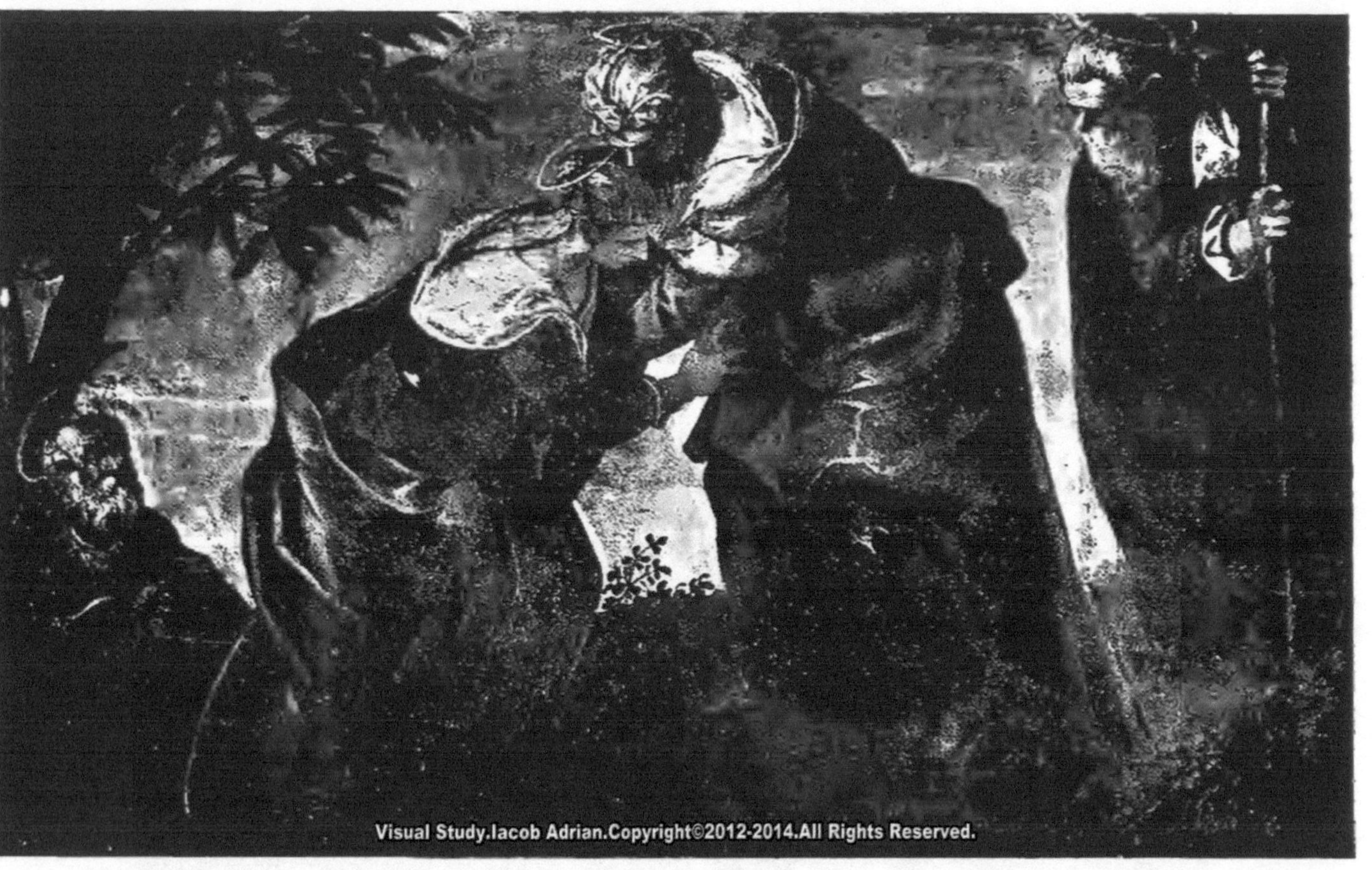

The Visitation (*St. Roche's, Venice*)

Mariä Heimsuchung (*Venedig, Rochuskirche*)

La Visitation (*Église St-Roch, Venise*)

D. Anderson, Photo.

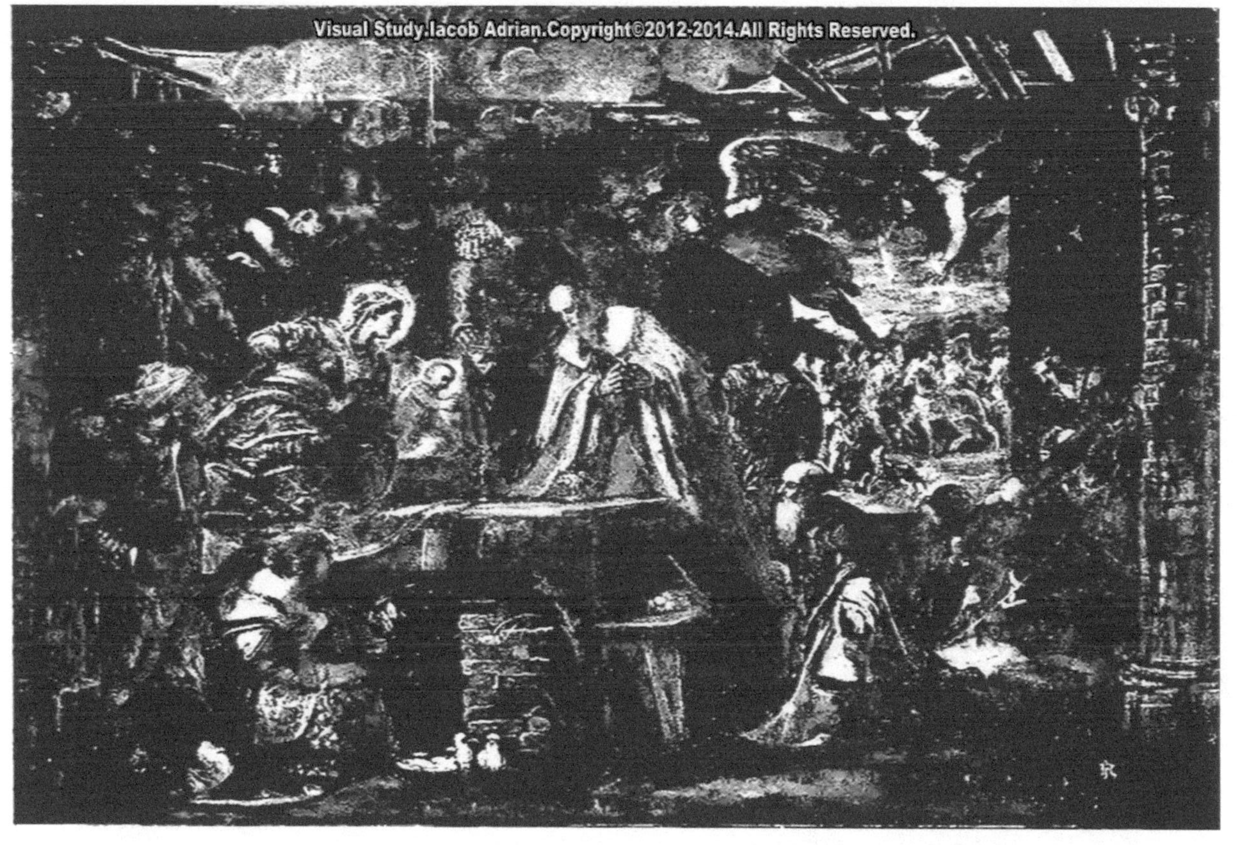

THE ADORATION OF THE MAGI
(*St. Roche's, Venice*)

DIE ANBETUNG DER WEISEN
(*Venedig, Rochuskirche*)
D. Anderson, Photo.

L'ADORATION DES MAGES
(*Église St-Roch, Venise*)

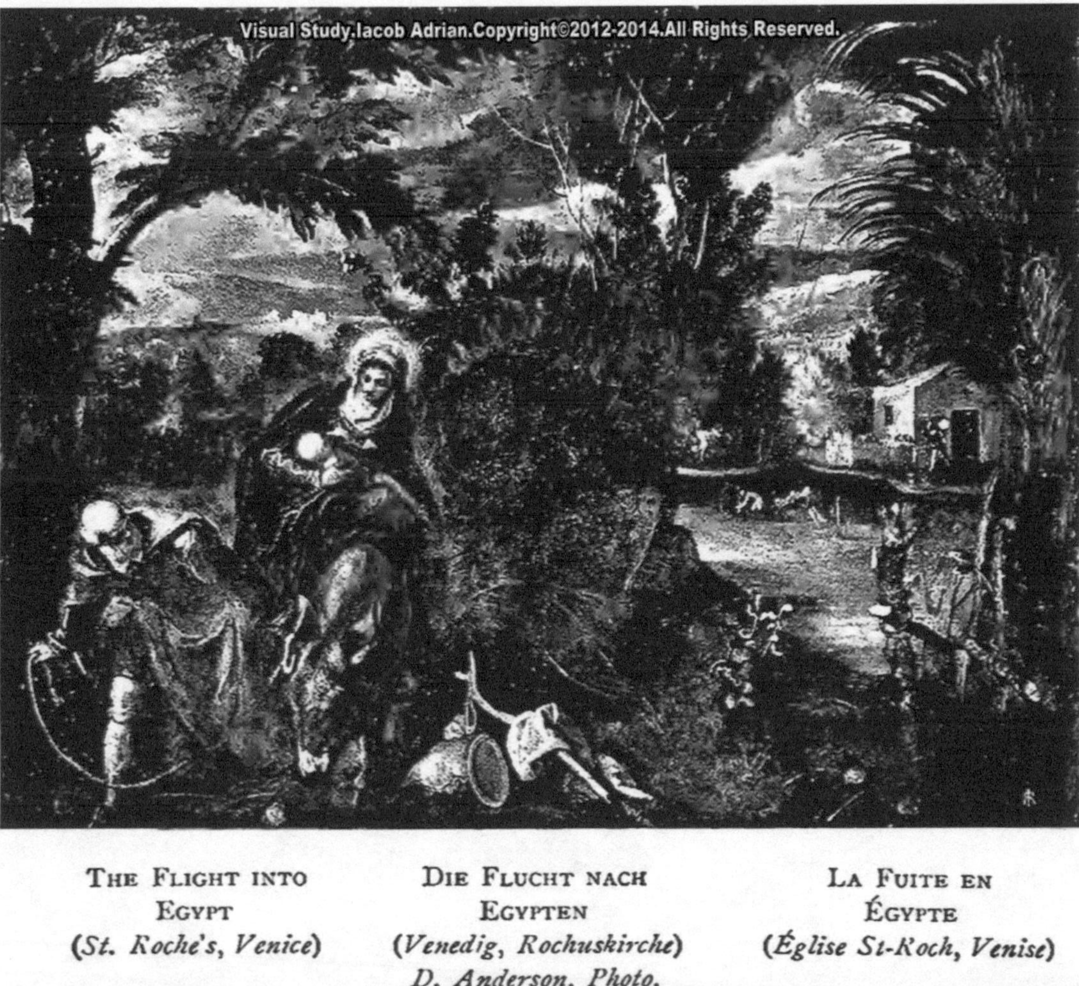

THE FLIGHT INTO EGYPT
(*St. Roche's, Venice*)

DIE FLUCHT NACH EGYPTEN
(*Venedig, Rochuskirche*)

LA FUITE EN ÉGYPTE
(*Église St-Roch, Venise*)

D. Anderson, Photo.

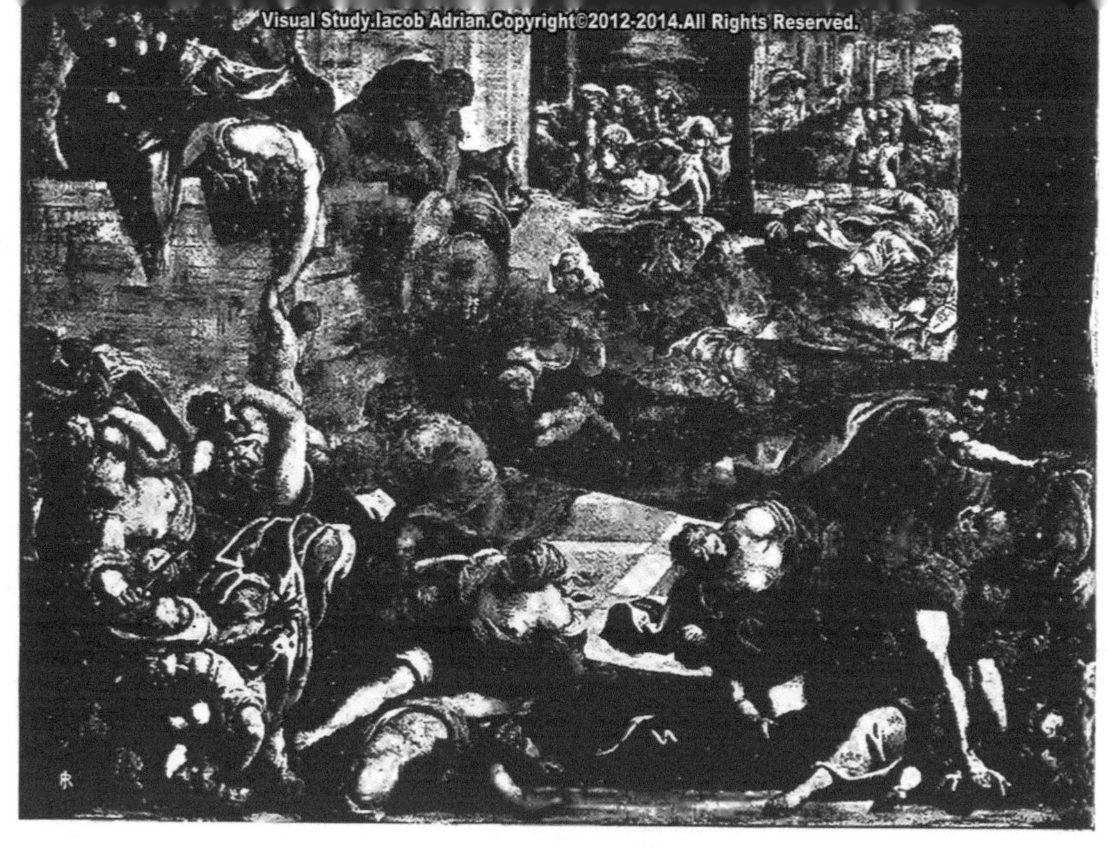

THE MASSACRE OF THE INNOCENTS
(*St. Roche's, Venice*)

MORD DER UNSCHULDIGEN KINDLEIN
(*Venedig, Rochuskirche*)
D. Anderson, Photo.

LE MASSACRE DES INNOCENTS
(*Église St-Roch, Venise*)

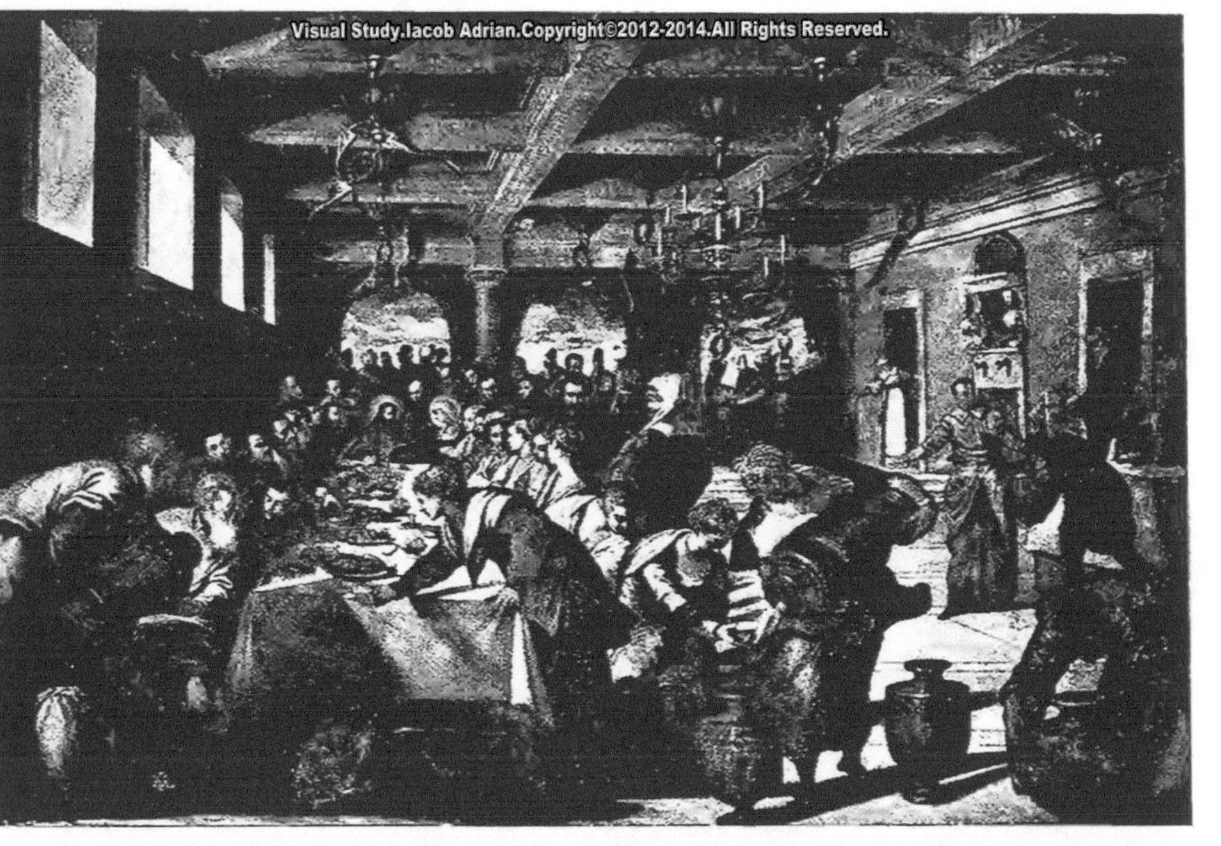

THE MARRIAGE AT CANA
(*S. Maria della Salute, Venice*)

LES NOCES DE CANA
(*S. Maria della Salute, Venise*)

DIE HOCHZEIT ZU KANA
(*Venedig, S. Maria della Salute*)

D. Anderson, Photo.

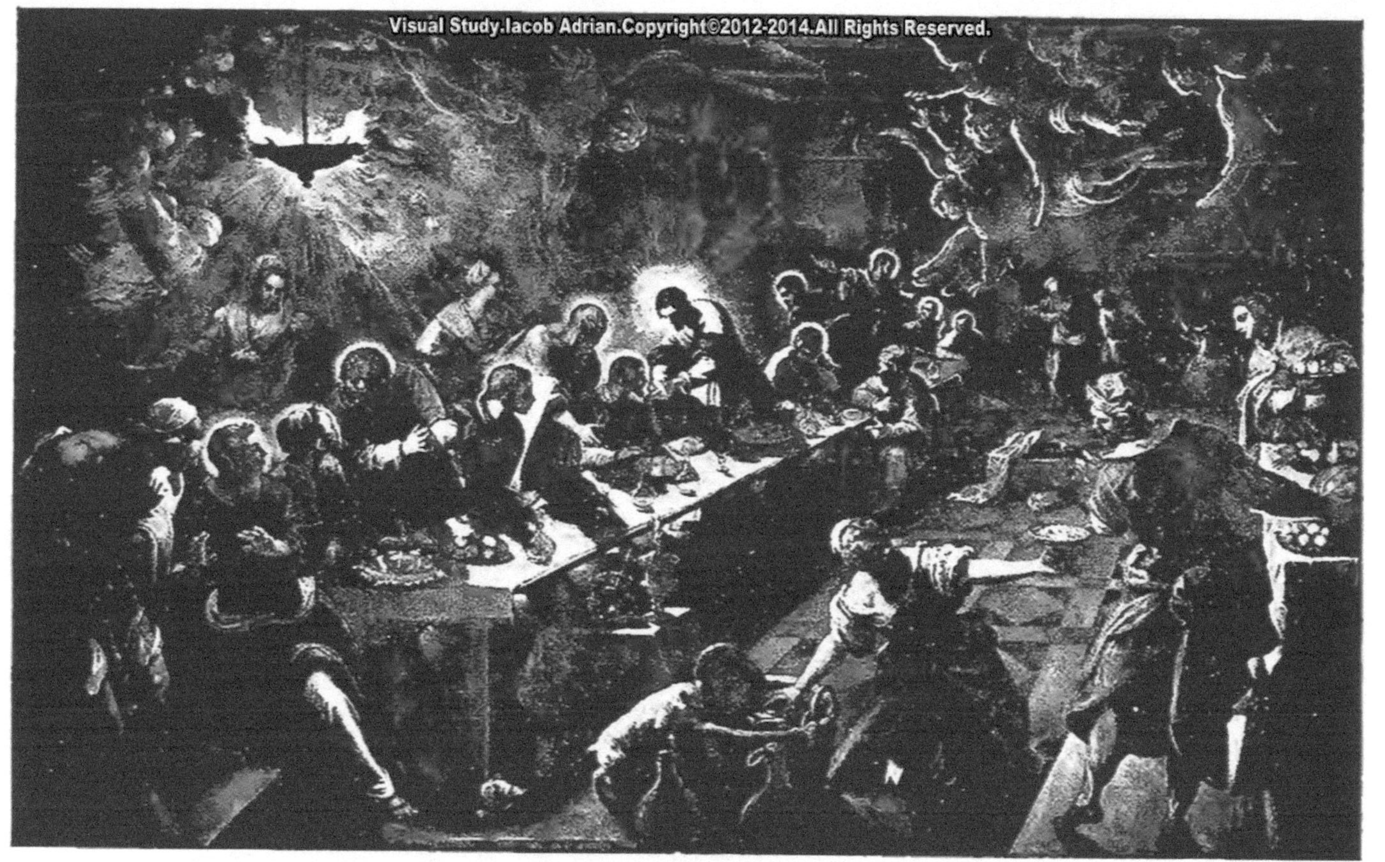

THE LAST SUPPER
(*S. Giorgio Maggiore, Venice*)

DAS HL. ABENDMAHL
(*Venedig, S. Giorgio Maggiore*)

LA SAINTE CÈNE
(*S. Giorgio Maggiore, Venise*)

D. Anderson, Photo.

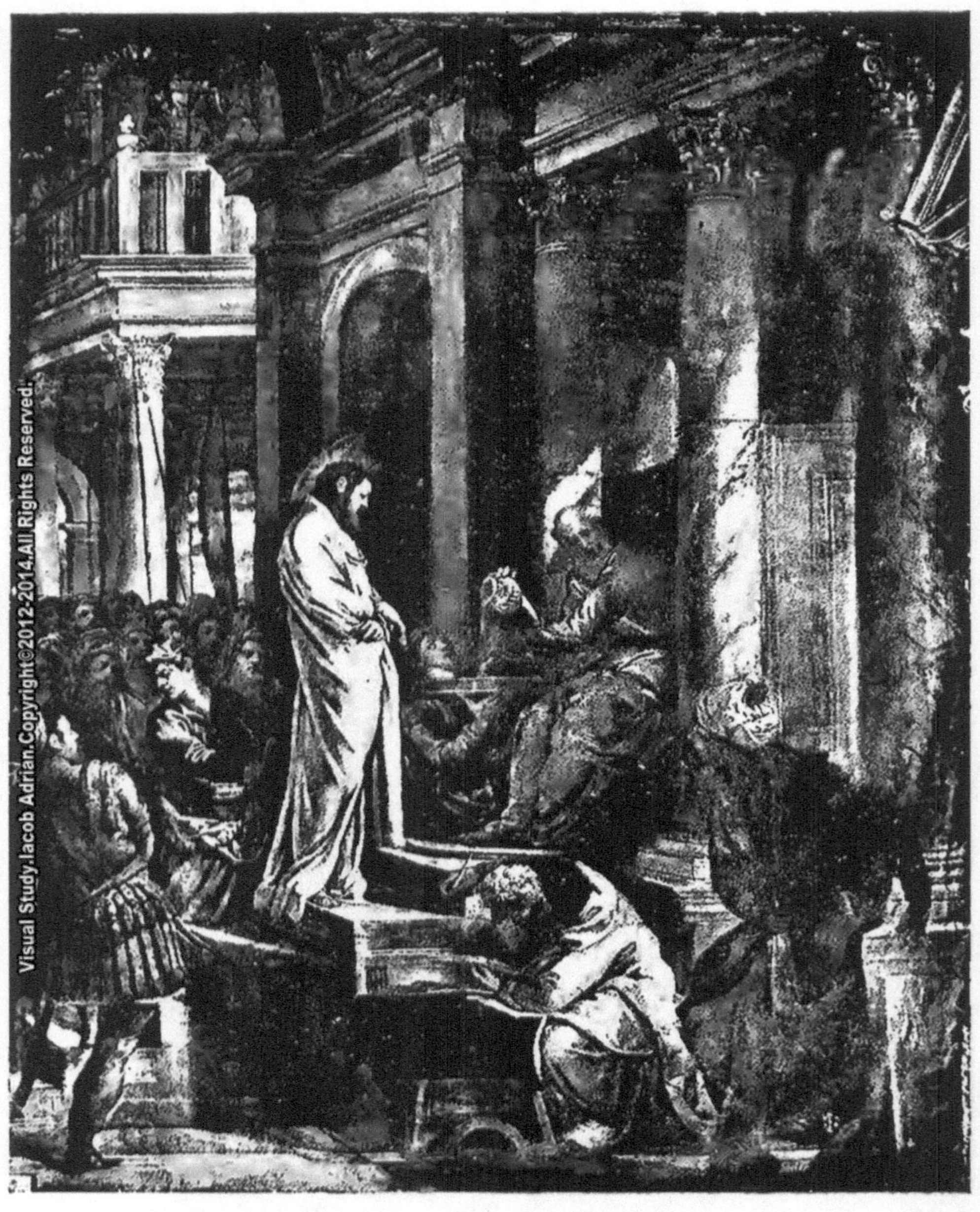

CHRIST BEFORE PILATE
(*St. Roche's, Venice*)

LE CHRIST DEVANT PILATE
(*Église St-Roch, Venise*)

CHRISTUS VOR PILATUS
(*Venedig, Rochuskirche*)

D. Anderson, Photo.

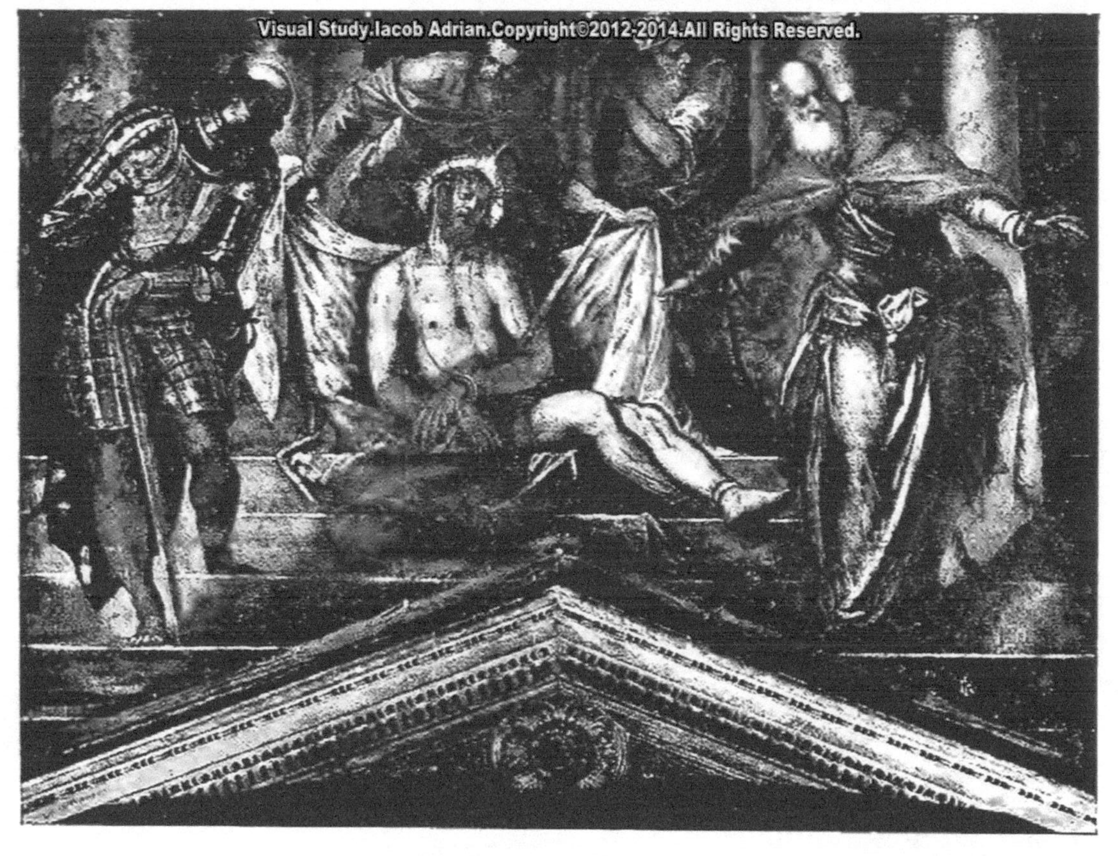

CHRIST CROWNED WITH THORNS
(*St. Roche's, Venice*)

DIE DORNENKRÖNUNG CHRISTI
(*Venedig, Rochuskirche*)
D. Anderson, Photo.

LE COURONNEMENT D'ÉPINES
(*Église St-Roch, Venise*)

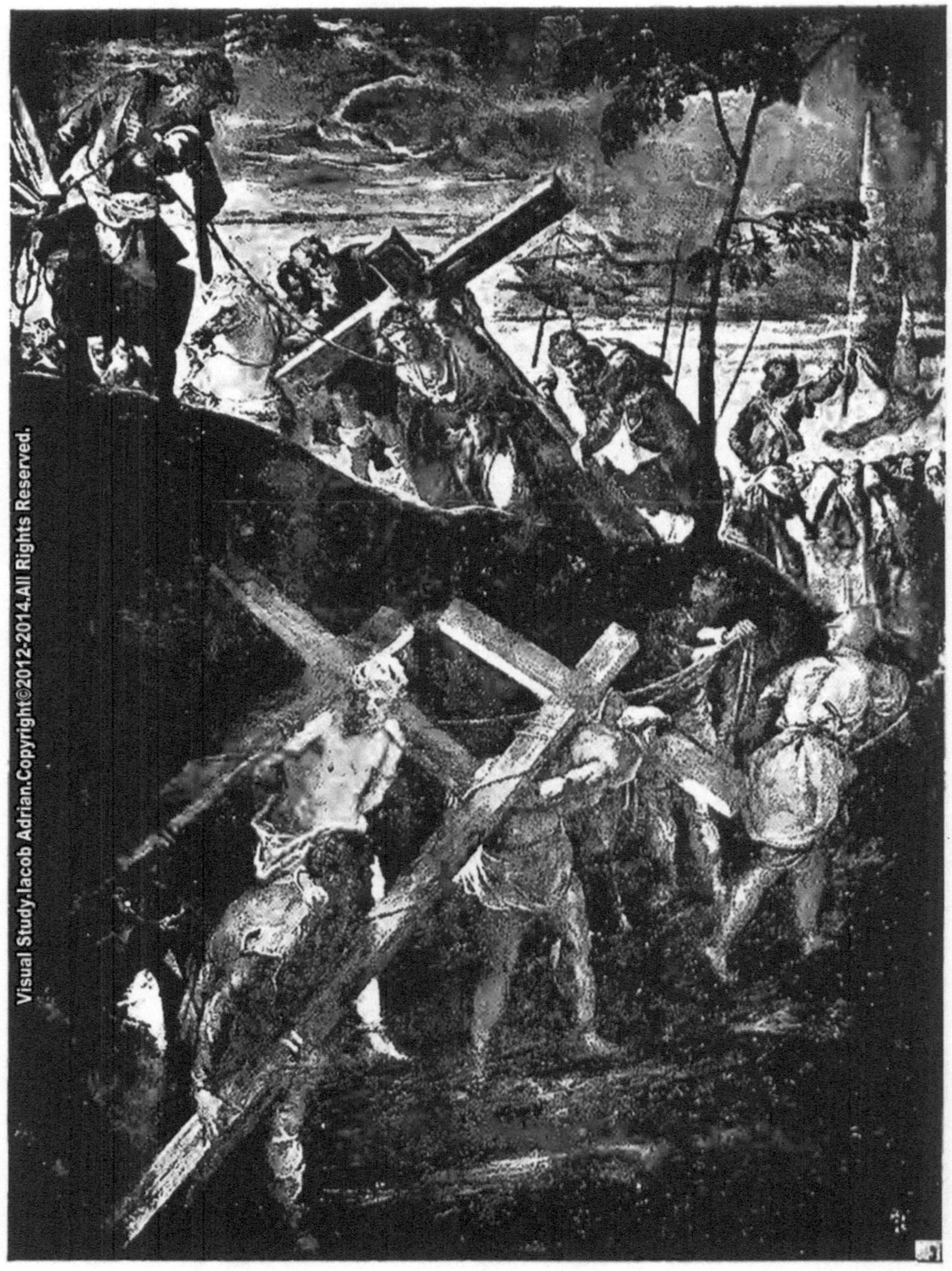

CHRIST BEARING THE CROSS
(*St. Roche's, Venice*)

JÉSUS PORTANT LA CROIX
(*Église St-Roch, Venise*)

DIE KREUZTRAGUNG
(*Venedig, Rochuskirche*) *D. Anderson, Photo.*

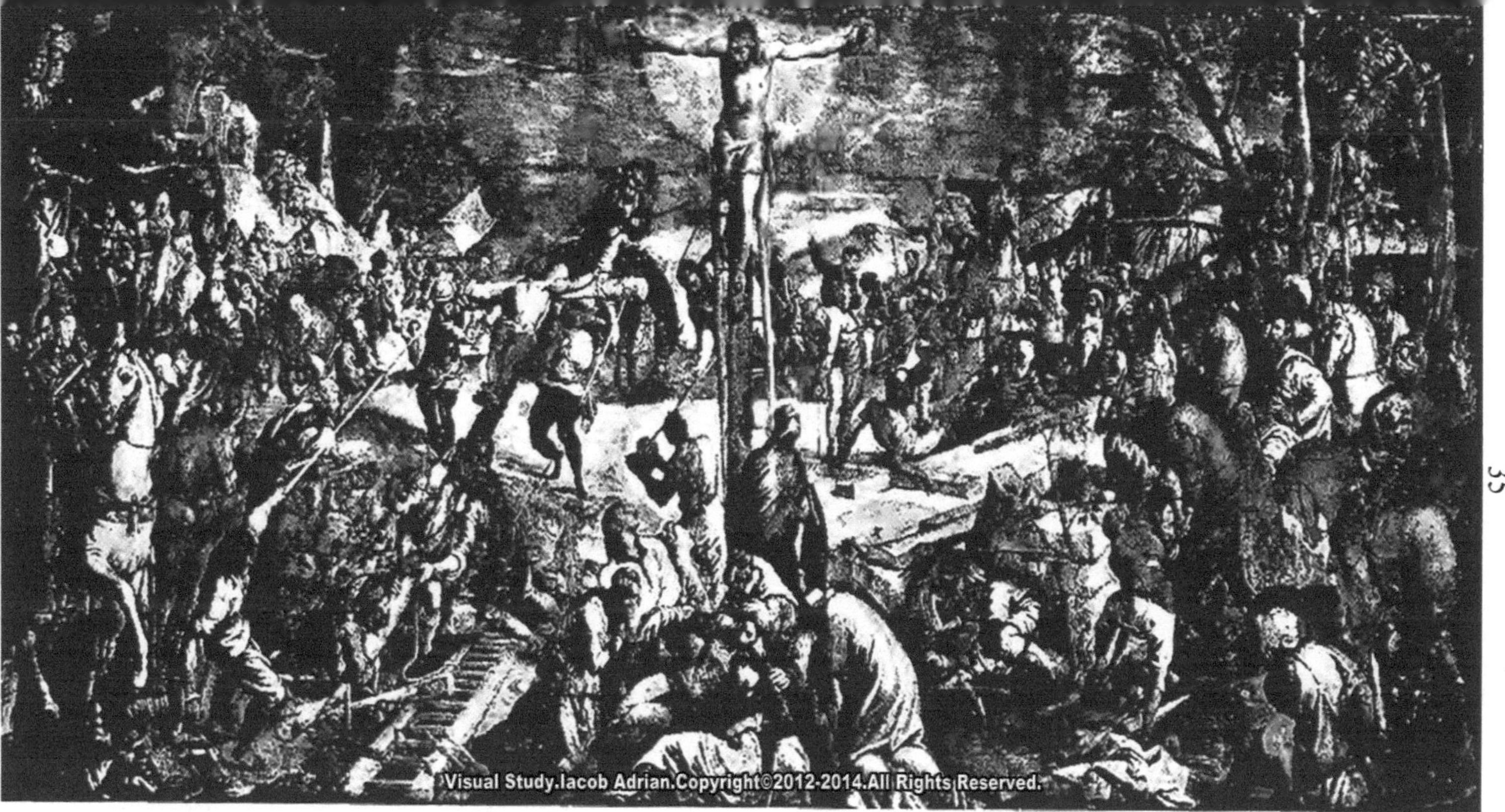

THE CRUCIFIXION
(*St. Roche's, Venice*)

DIE KREUZIGUNG
(*Venedig, Rochuskirche*)
D. Anderson, Photo.

LE CRUCIFIEMENT
(*Église St-Roch, Venise*)

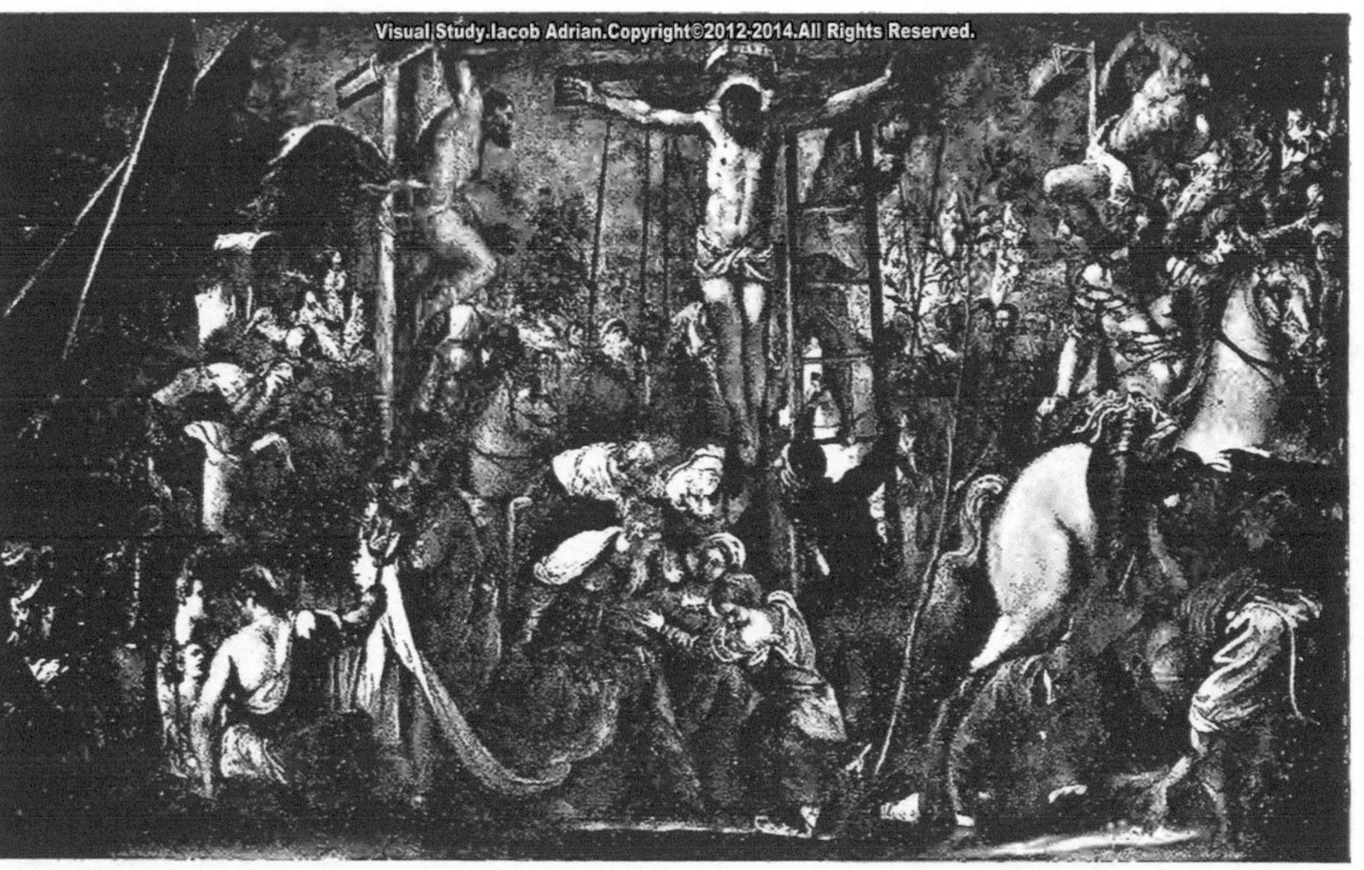

THE CRUCIFIXION
(*Academy, Venice*)

DIE KREUZIGUNG
(*Venedig, Akademie*)

LE CRUCIFIEMENT
(*Académie, Venise*)

F. Hanfstaengl, Photo.

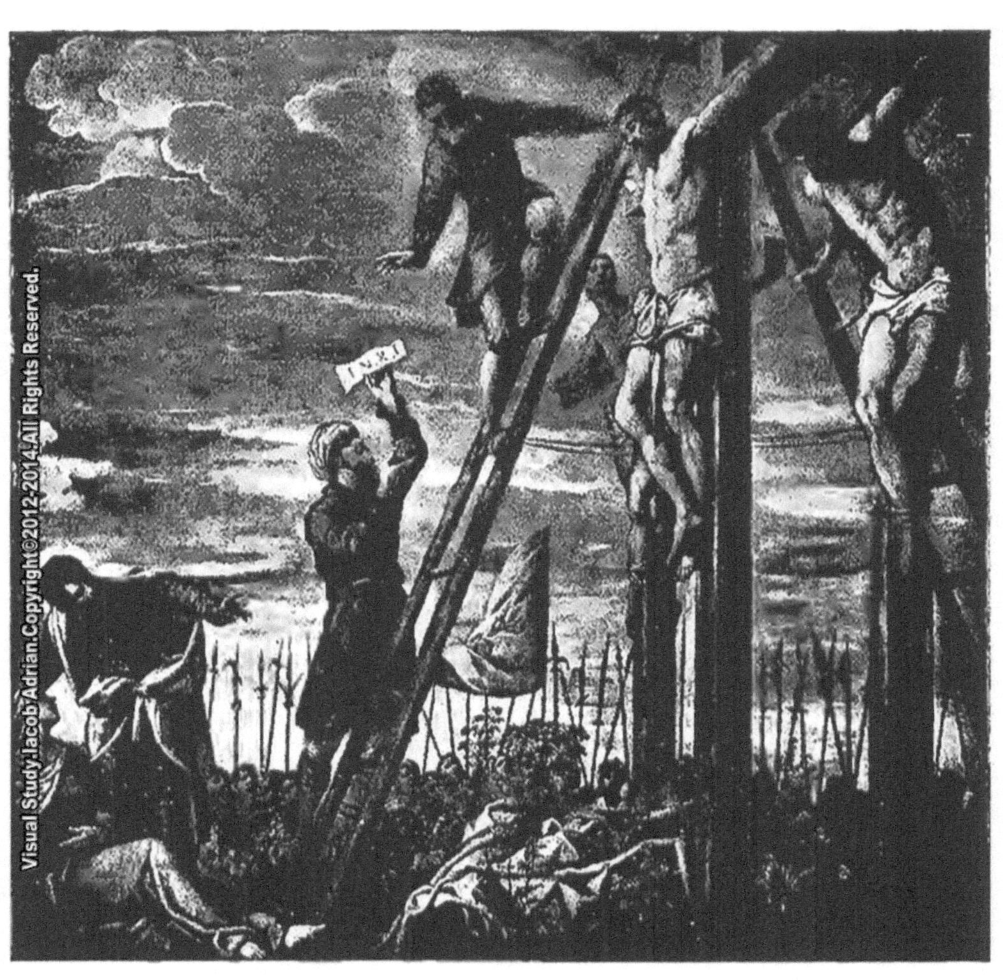

THE CRUCIFIXION (*S. Cassiano, Venice*)

DIE KREUZIGUNG (*Venedig, S. Cassiano*)

LE CRUCIFIEMENT (*S. Cassiano, Venise*)

D. Anderson, Photo.

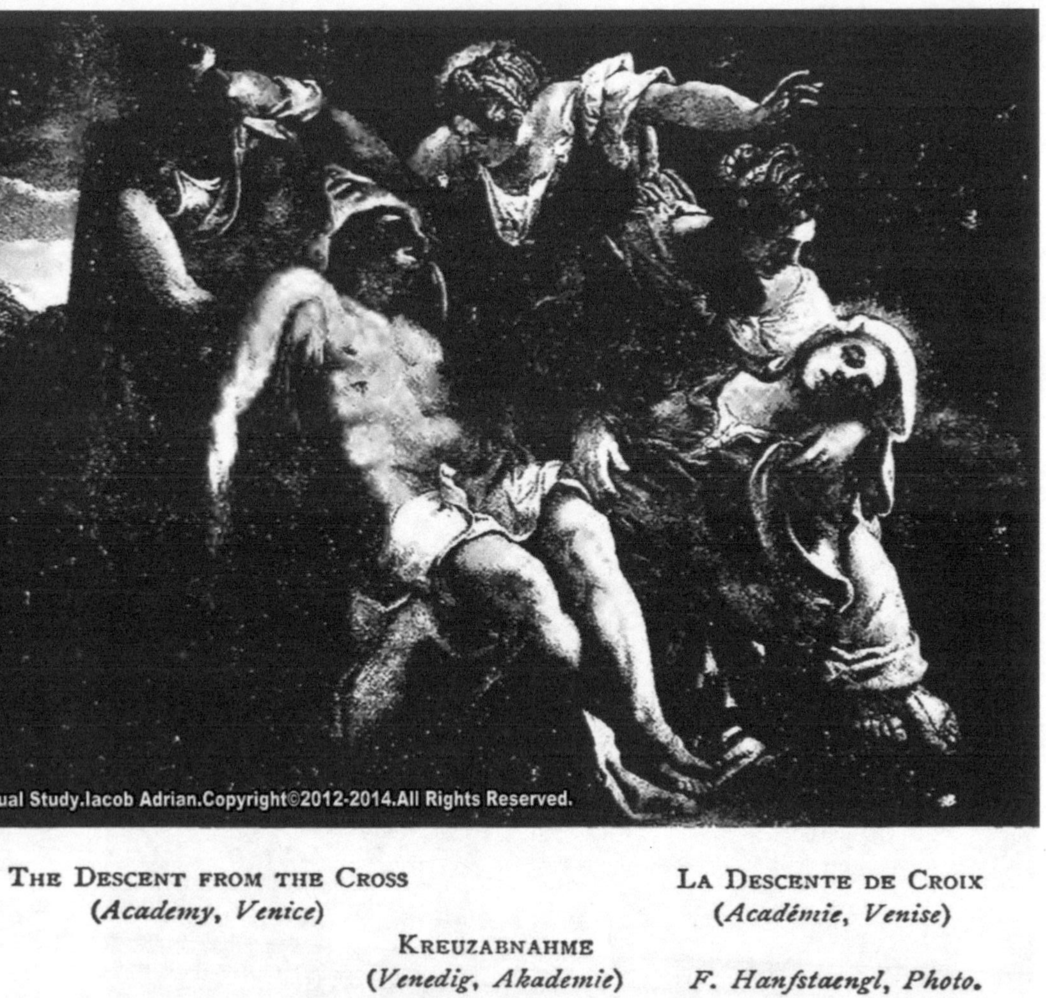

THE DESCENT FROM THE CROSS
(*Academy, Venice*)

LA DESCENTE DE CROIX
(*Académie, Venise*)

KREUZABNAHME
(*Venedig, Akademie*)

F. Hanfstaengl, Photo.

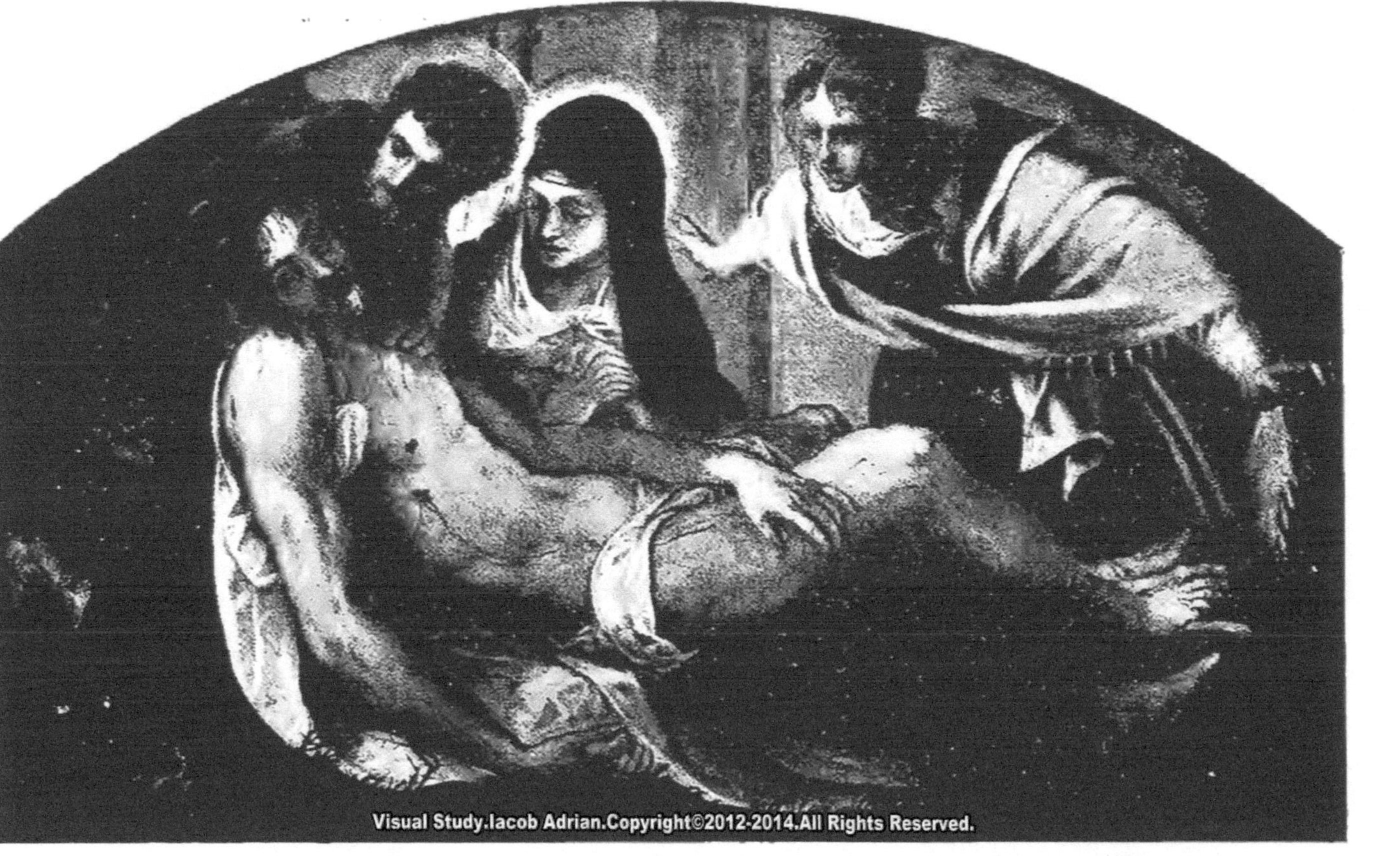

THE MOURNING FOR CHRIST
(*Pinacotheca, Milan*)

BEWEINUNG CHRISTI
(*Mailand, Pinakothek*)
F. Hanfstaengl, Photo.

LE CHRIST PLEURÉ
(*Pinacothèque, Milan*)

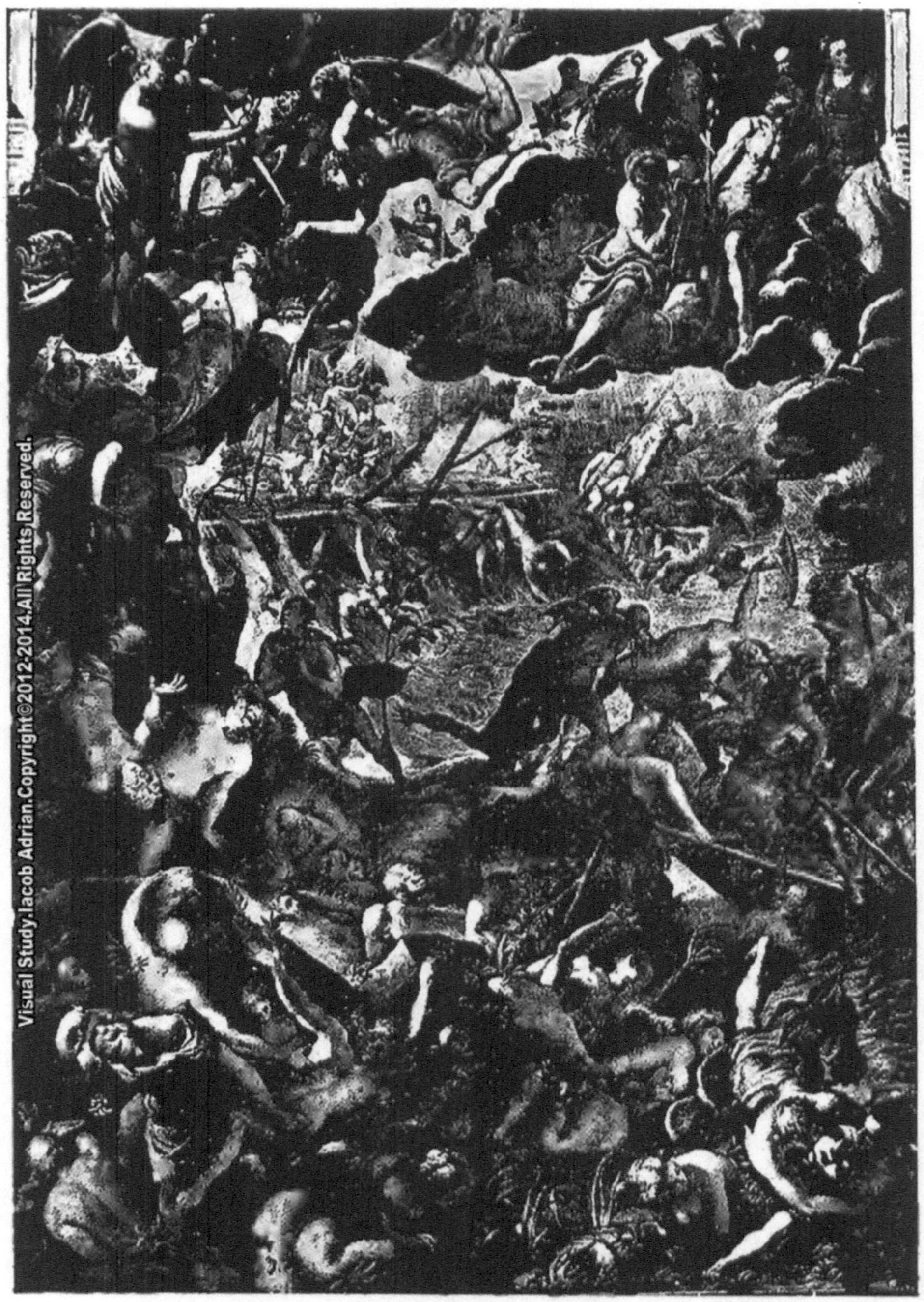

THE LAST JUDGMENT
(*S. Maria dell' Orto, Venice*)

LE DERNIER JUGEMENT
(*S. Maria dell' Orto, Venise*)

DAS JÜNGSTE GERICHT
(*Venedig, S. Maria dell' Orto*)

D. Anderson, Photo.

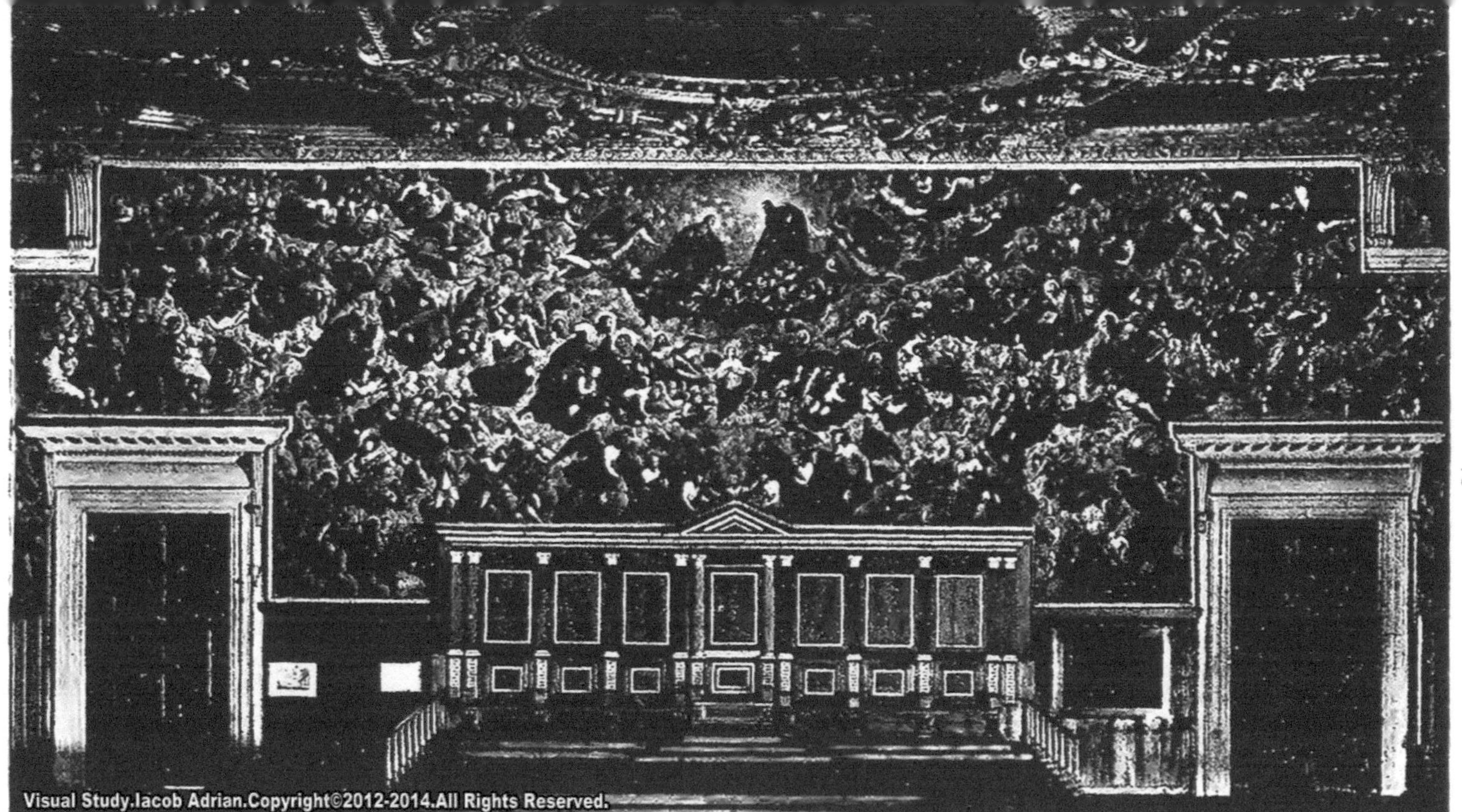

PARADISE
(*Doge's Palace, Venice*)

PARADIES
(*Venedig, Dogenpalast*)
D. Anderson, Photo.

LE PARADIS
(*Palais ducal, Venise*)

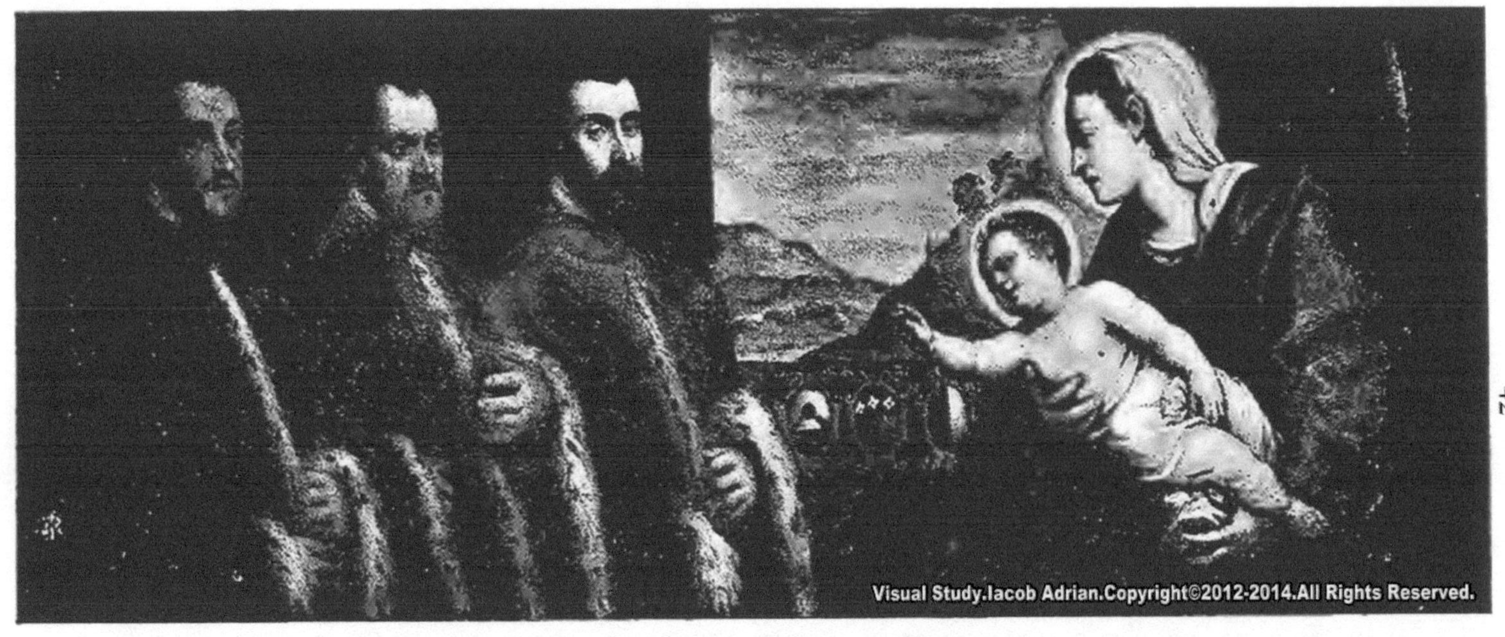

THE VIRGIN AND CHILD WITH THREE PORTRAITS
(Academy, Venice)

LA VIERGE ET L'ENFANT AVEC TROIS PORTRAITS
(Académie, Venise)

MARIA MIT DEM KINDE UND DREI BILDNISSEN
(Venedig, Akademie)

D. Anderson, Photo.

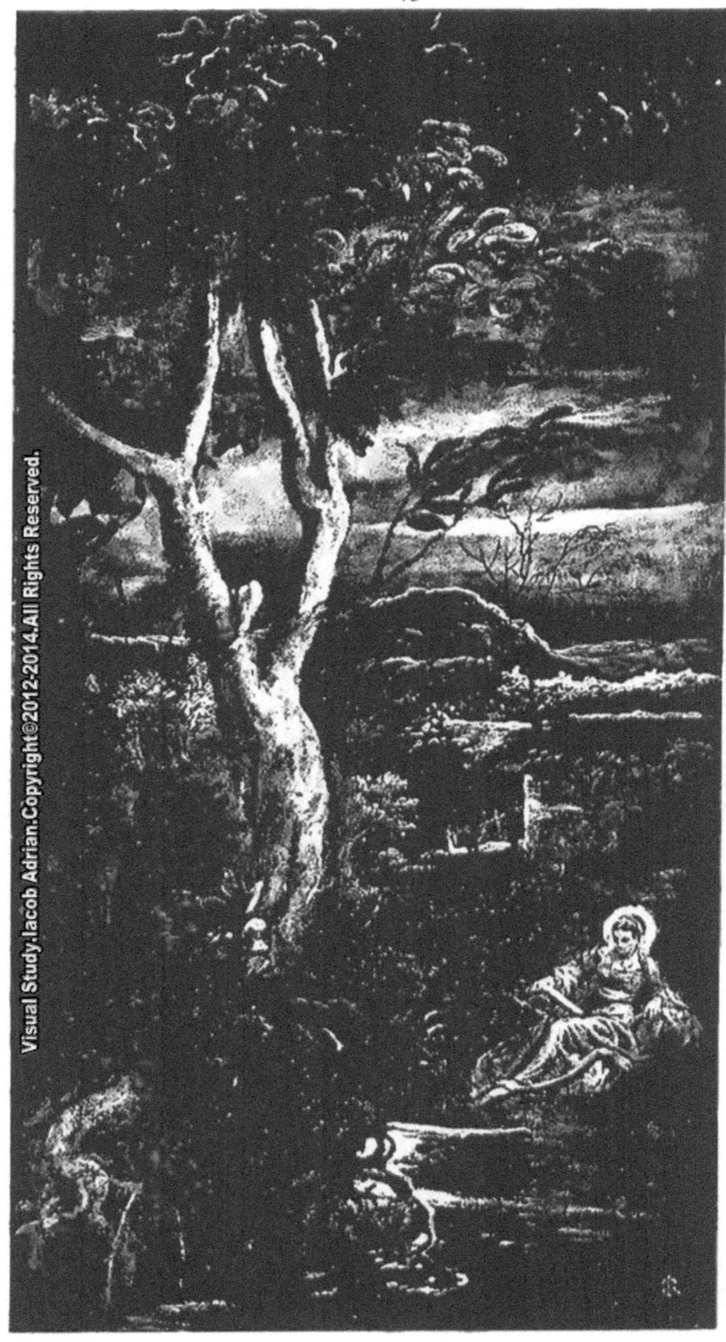

MARY MAGDALENE
(*St. Roche's, Venice*)

LA MADELEINE
(*Église St-Roch, Venise*)

MAGDALENA
(*Venedig, Rochuskirche*)

D. Anderson, Photo.

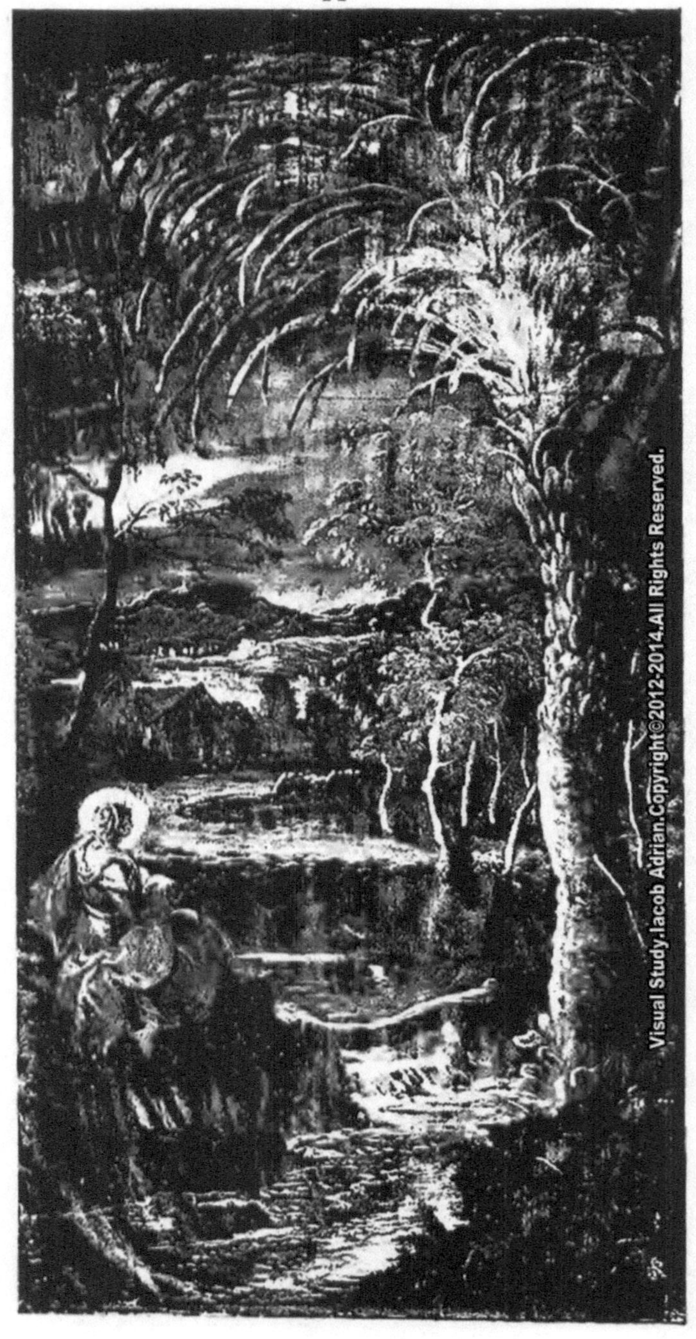

St. Mary the Egyptian
(*St. Roche's, Venice*)

Ste Marie l'Égyptienne
(*Église St-Roch, Venise*)

Die hl. Maria die Ägypterin
(*Venedig, Rochuskirche*)

D. Anderson, Photo.

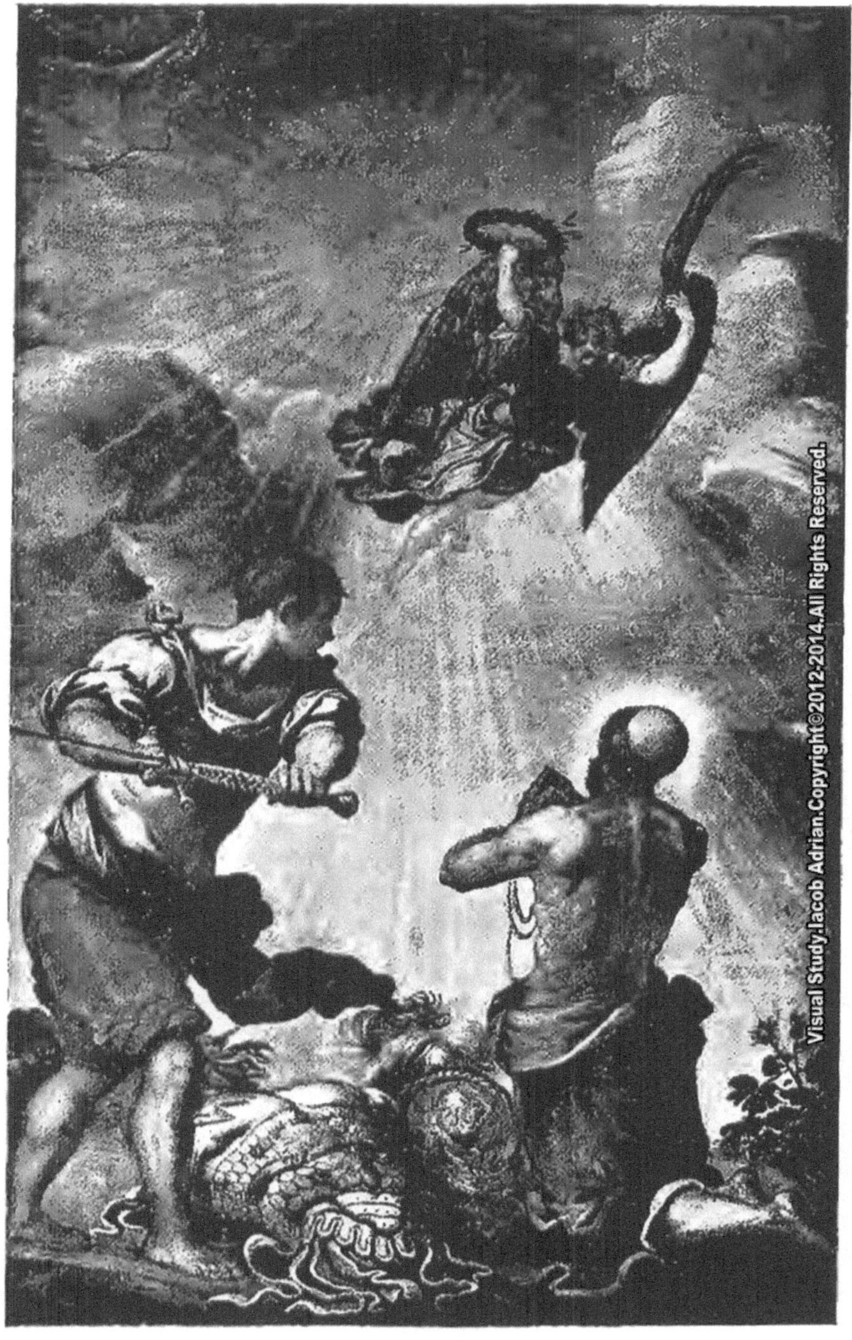

THE DECAPITATION OF ST. PAUL
(*S. Maria dell' Orto, Venice*)

LA DÉCAPITATION DE ST PAUL
(*S. Maria dell' Orto, Venise*)

DIE ENTHAUPTUNG DES HL. PAULUS
(*Venedig, S. Maria dell' Orto*) *D. Anderson, Photo.*

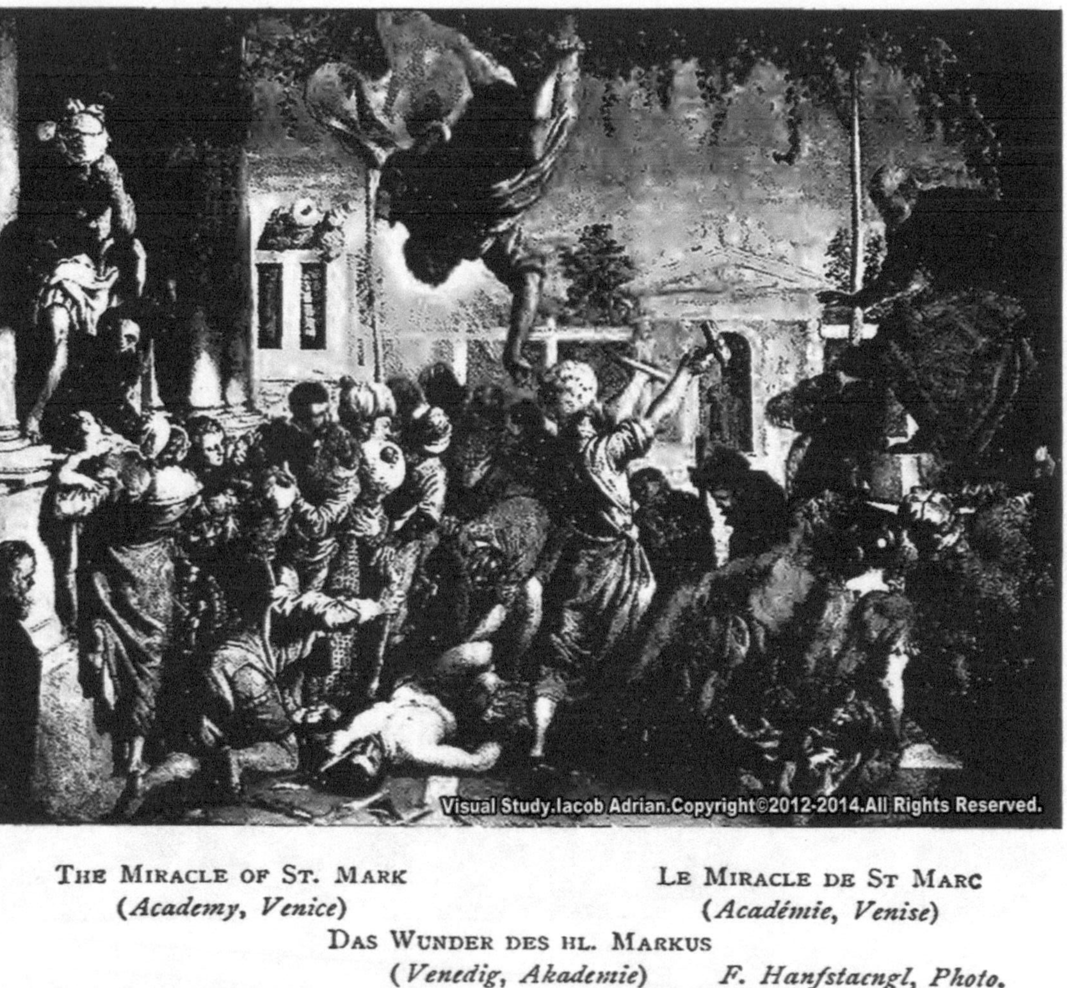

The Miracle of St. Mark
(Academy, Venice)

Le Miracle de St Marc
(Académie, Venise)

Das Wunder des hl. Markus
(Venedig, Akademie)

F. Hanfstaengl, Photo.

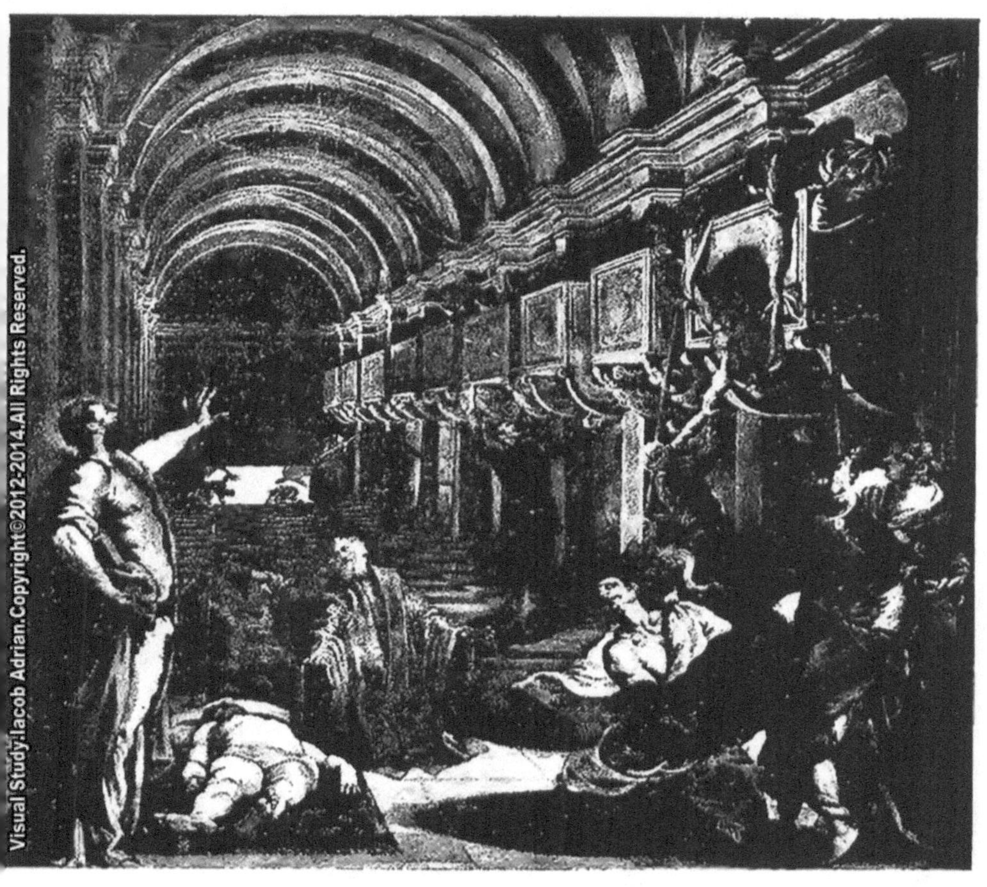

DISCOVERY OF THE BODY OF ST. MARK
(*Pinacotheca, Milan*)

DÉCOUVERTE DU CORPS DE ST MARC
(*Pinacothèque, Milan*)

AUFFINDUNG DES LEICHNAMS DES HL. MARKUS
(*Mailand, Pinakothek*)

F. Hanfstaengl, Photo.

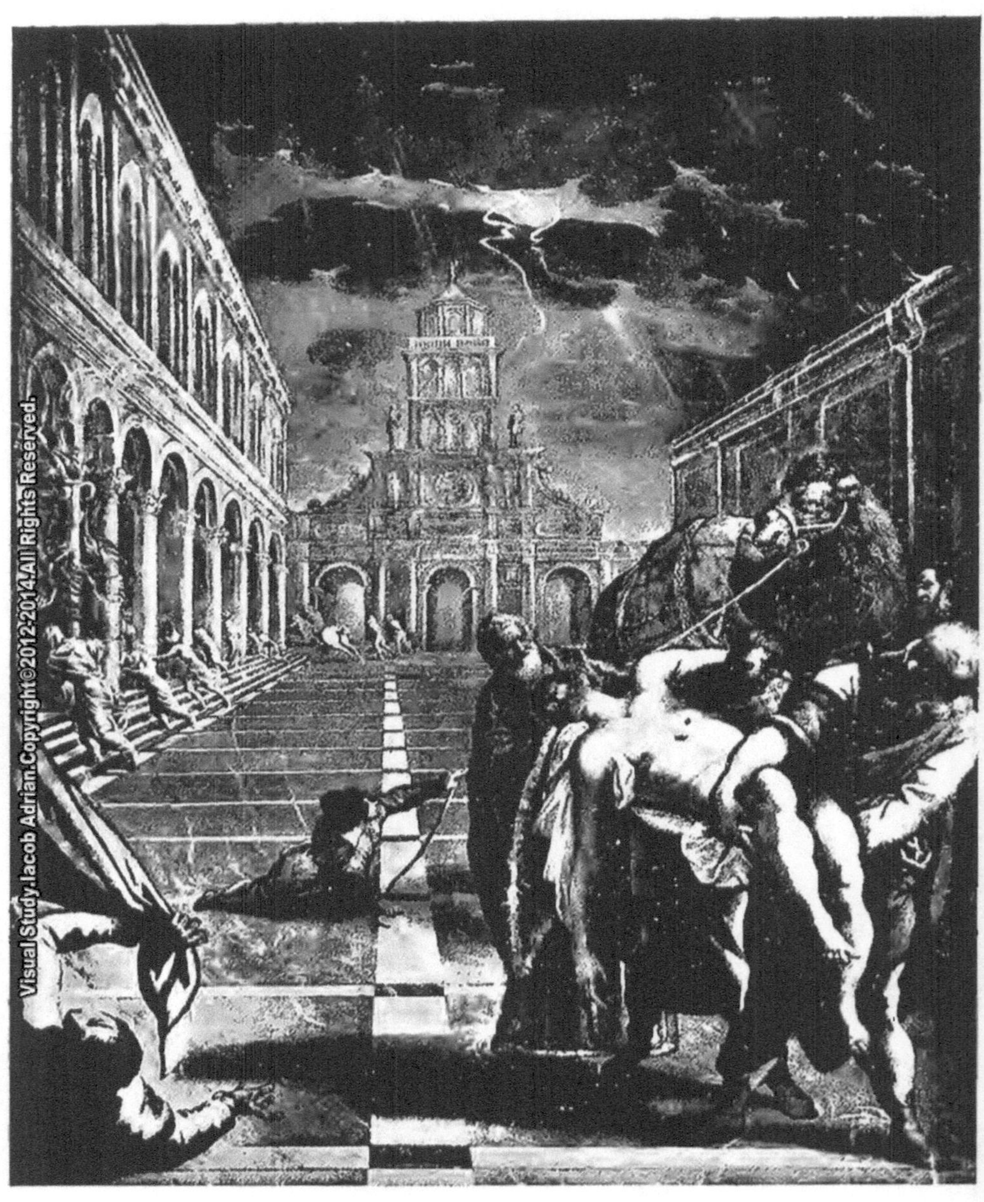

TRANSPORTATION OF THE BODY OF ST. MARK
(*Royal Palace, Venice*)

TRANSPORT DU CORPS DE ST MARC
(*Palais royale, Venise*)

FORTSCHAFFUNG DES LEICHNAMS DES HL. MARKUS
(*Venedig, Kgl. Schloss*) *Frat. Alinari, Photo*

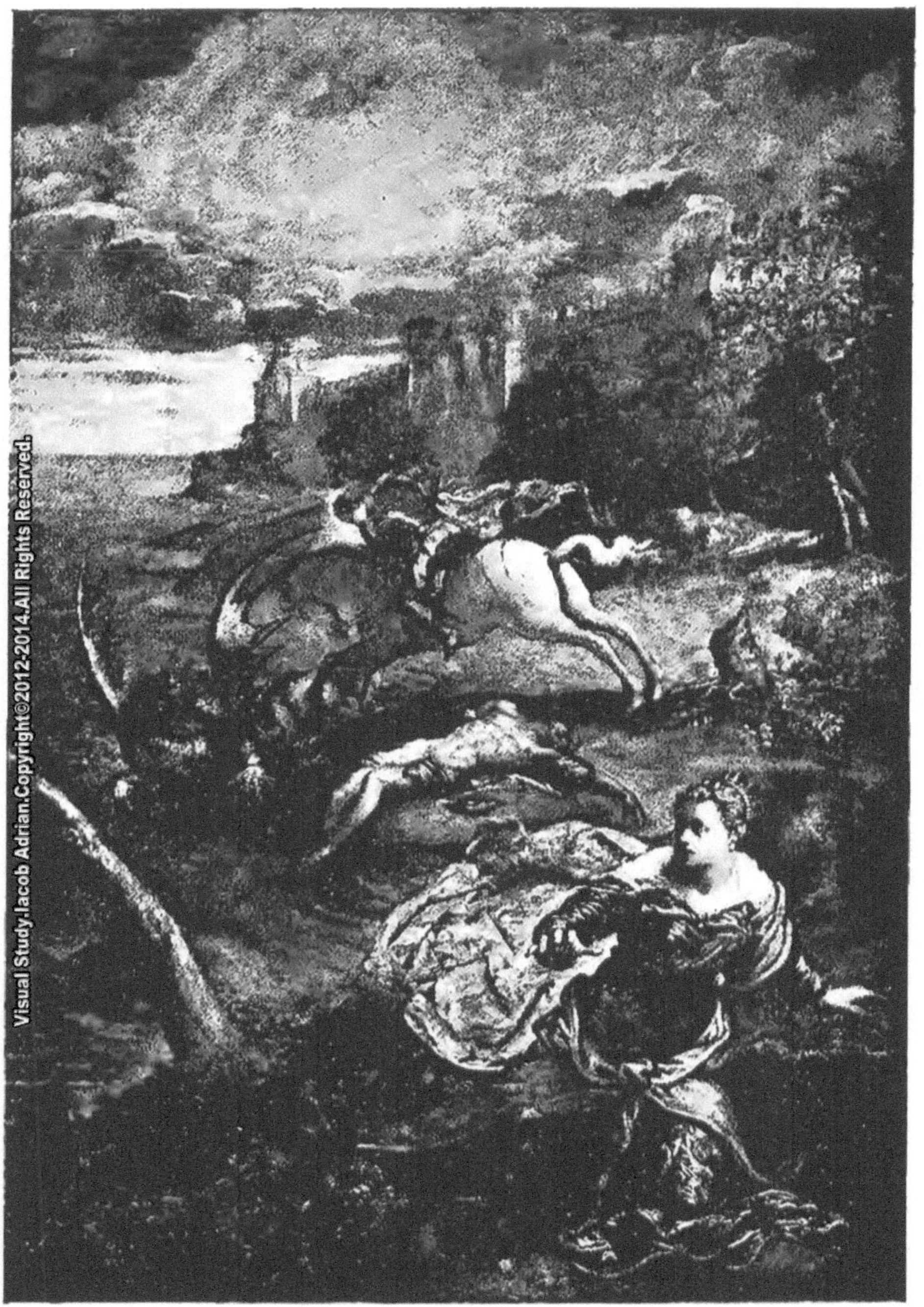

St. George and the Dragon (*National Gallery, London*)

St Georges et le Dragon (*Galerie nationale, Londres*)

Der hl. Georg und der Drache (*London, Nationalgalerie*)

F. Hanfstaengl, Photo.

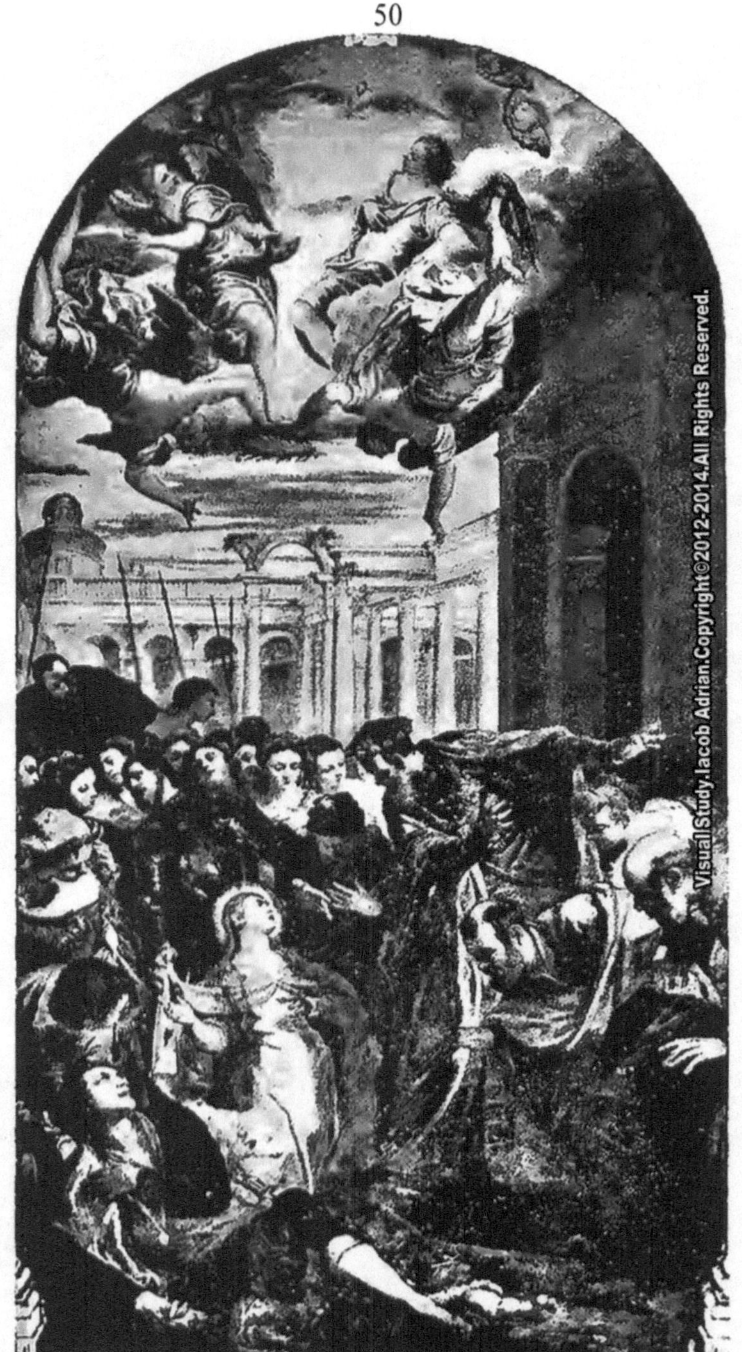

Martyrdom of St. Agnes
Maria dell' Orto, Venice)

Le Martyre de Ste Agnès
(S. Maria dell' Orto, Venise)

Das Märtertum der hl. Agnes
(Venedig, S. Maria dell' Orto) *D. Anderson, Photo.*

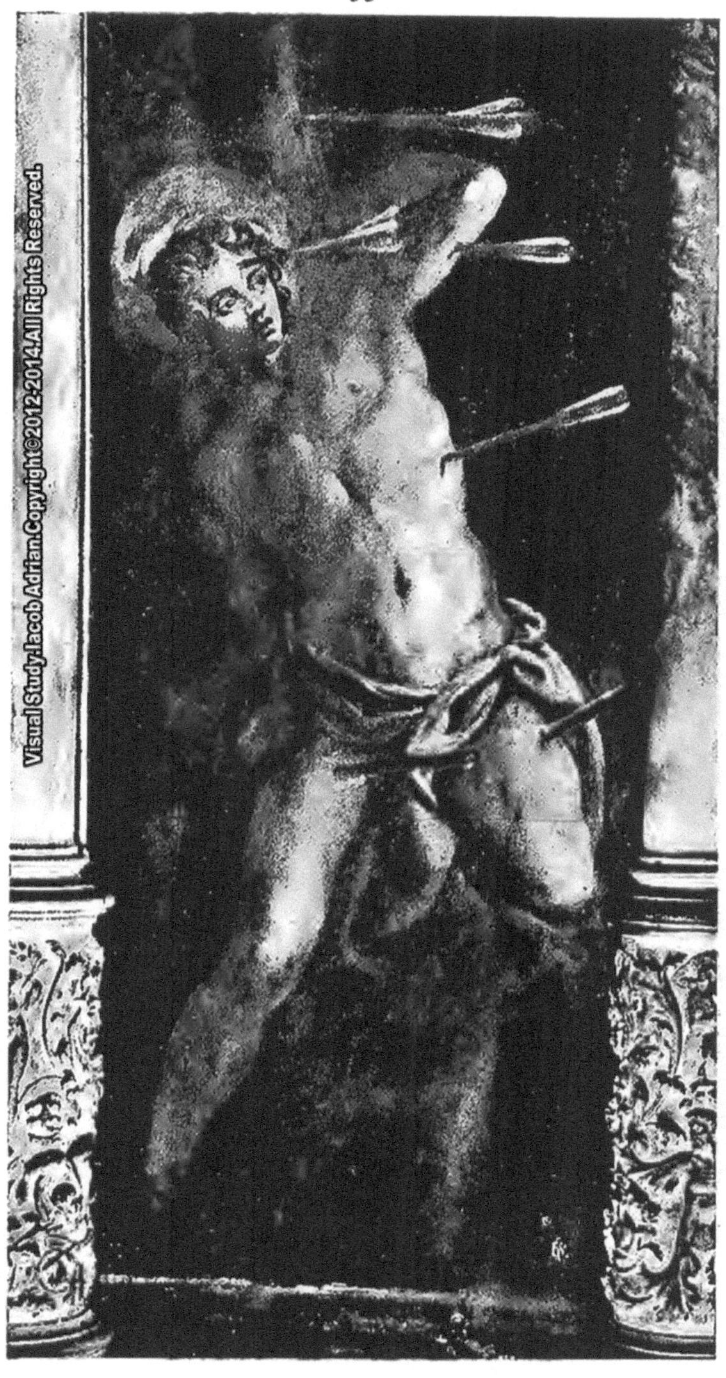

St. Sebastian
(*St. Roche's, Venice*)

St. Sebastian
(*Venedig, Rochuskirche*)
D. Anderson, Photo.

St Sébastien
(*Église St.-Roch, Venise*)

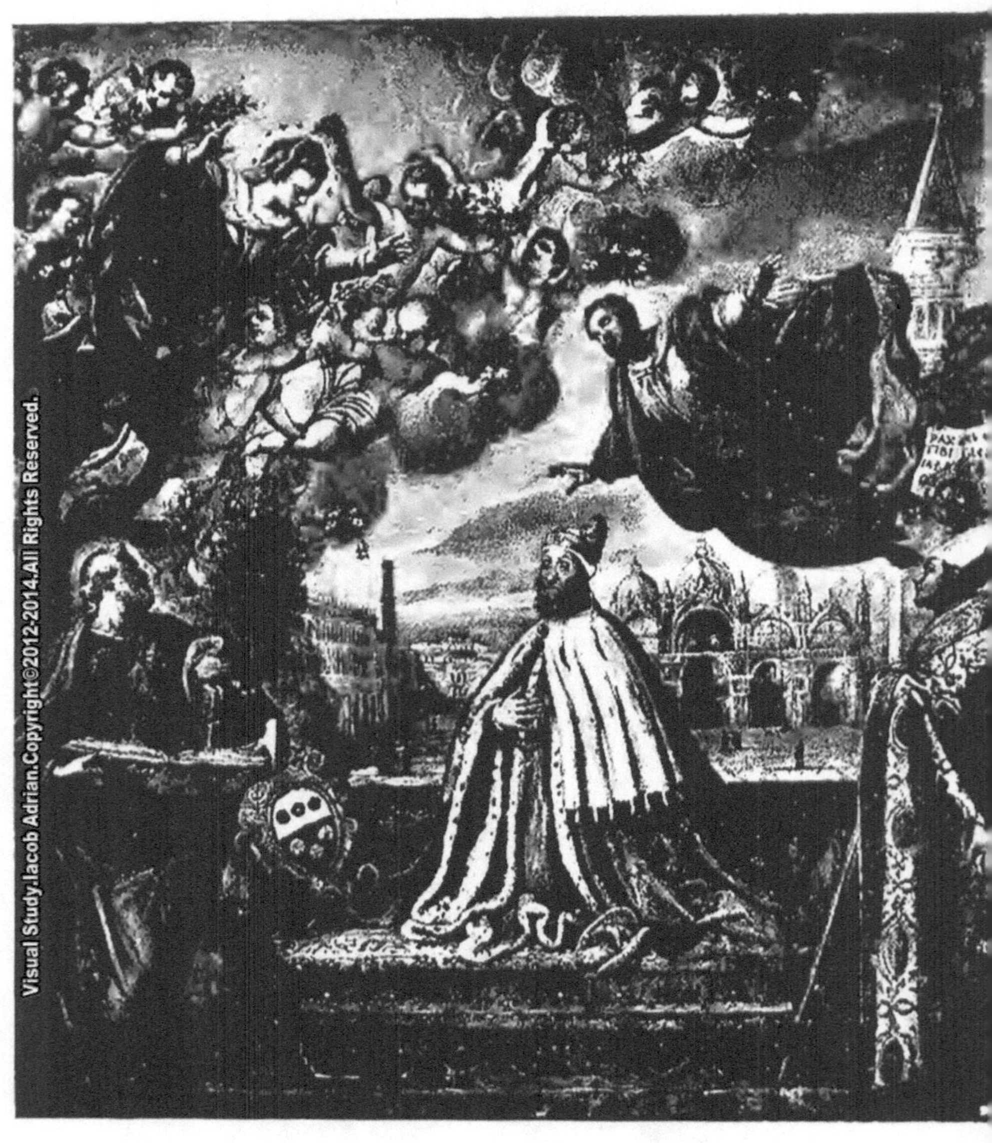

THE VIRGIN APPEARS TO
DOGE LOREDANO
(*Doge's Palace, Venice*)

LA VIERGE APPARAIT AU
DOGE LOREDANO
(*Palais ducal, Venise*)

MARIA ERSCHEINT DEM DOGEN LOREDANO
(*Venedig, Dogenpalast*)

D. Anderson, Photo.

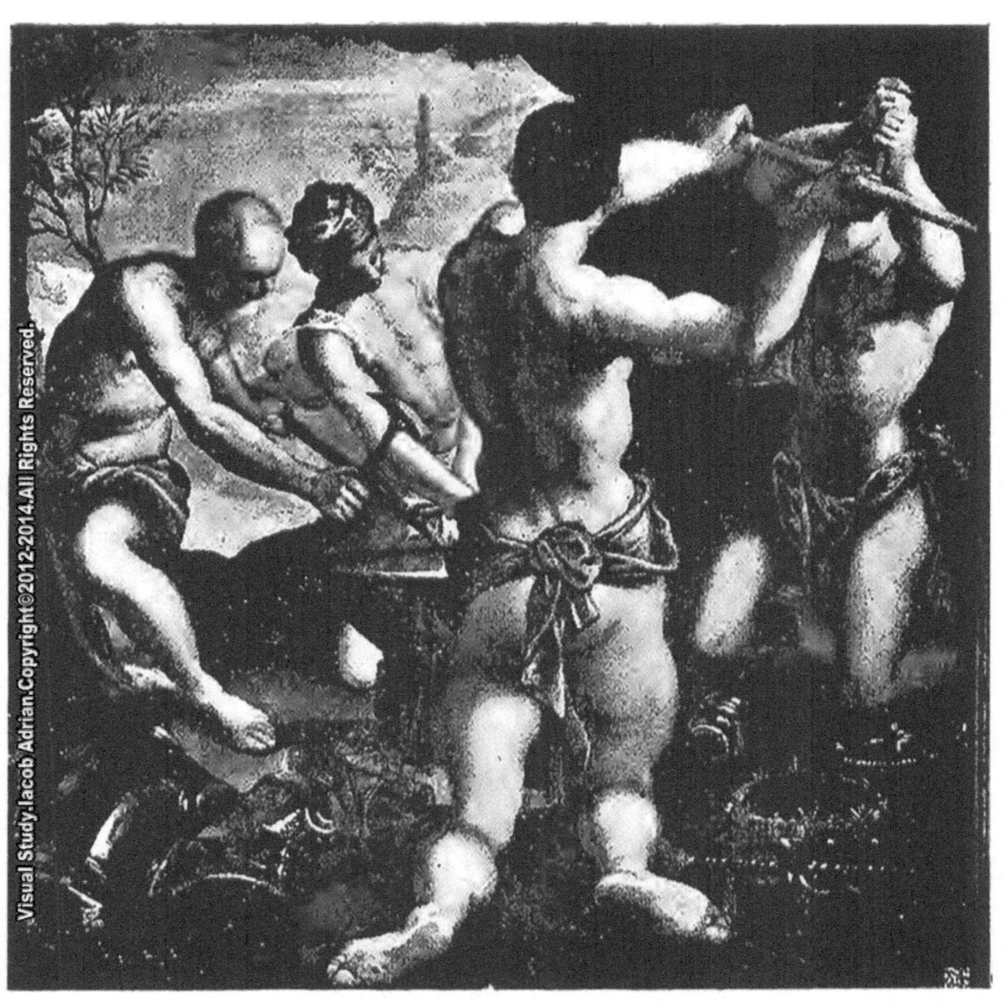

VULCAN'S FORGE
(*Doge's Palace, Venice*)

LA FORGE DE VULCAIN
(*Palais ducal, Venise*)

VULKANS SCHMIEDE
(*Venedig, Dogenpalast*)

D. Anderson, Photo.

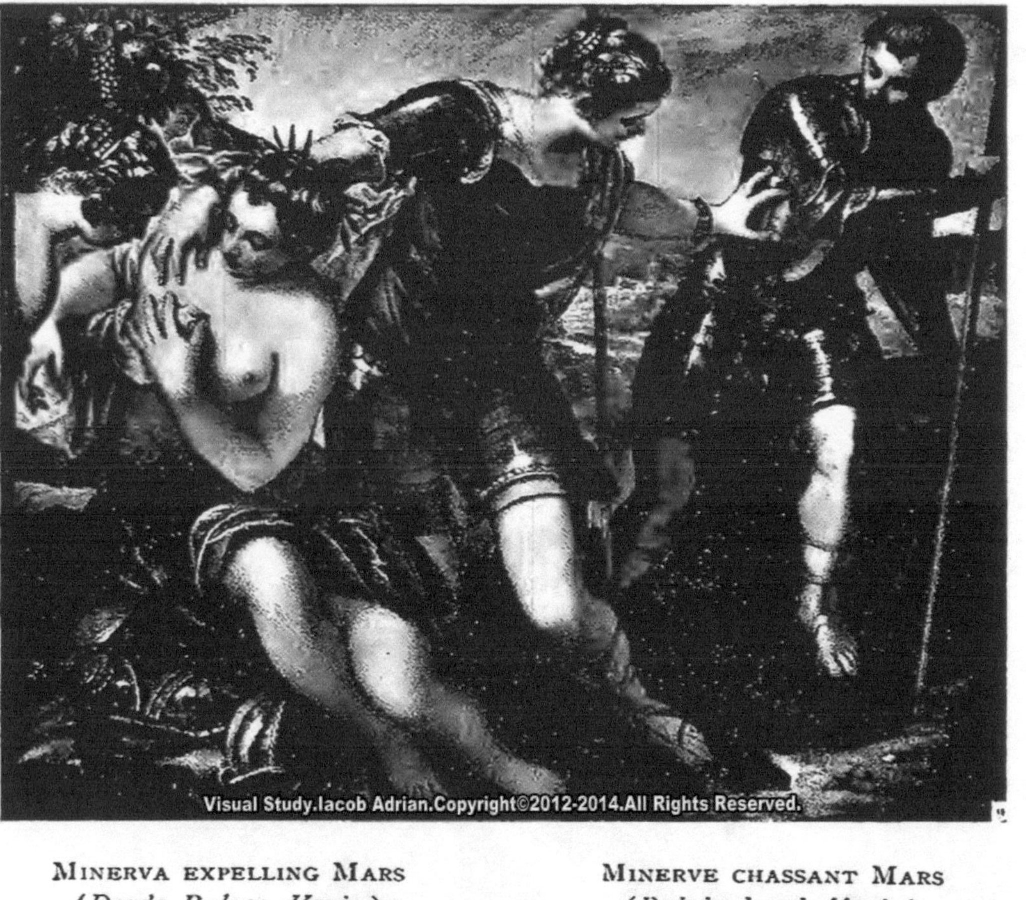

MINERVA EXPELLING MARS
(*Doge's Palace, Venice*)

MINERVE CHASSANT MARS
(*Palais ducal, Venise*)

MINERVA MARS AUSTREIBEND
(*Venedig, Dogenpalast*)

D. Anderson, Photo.

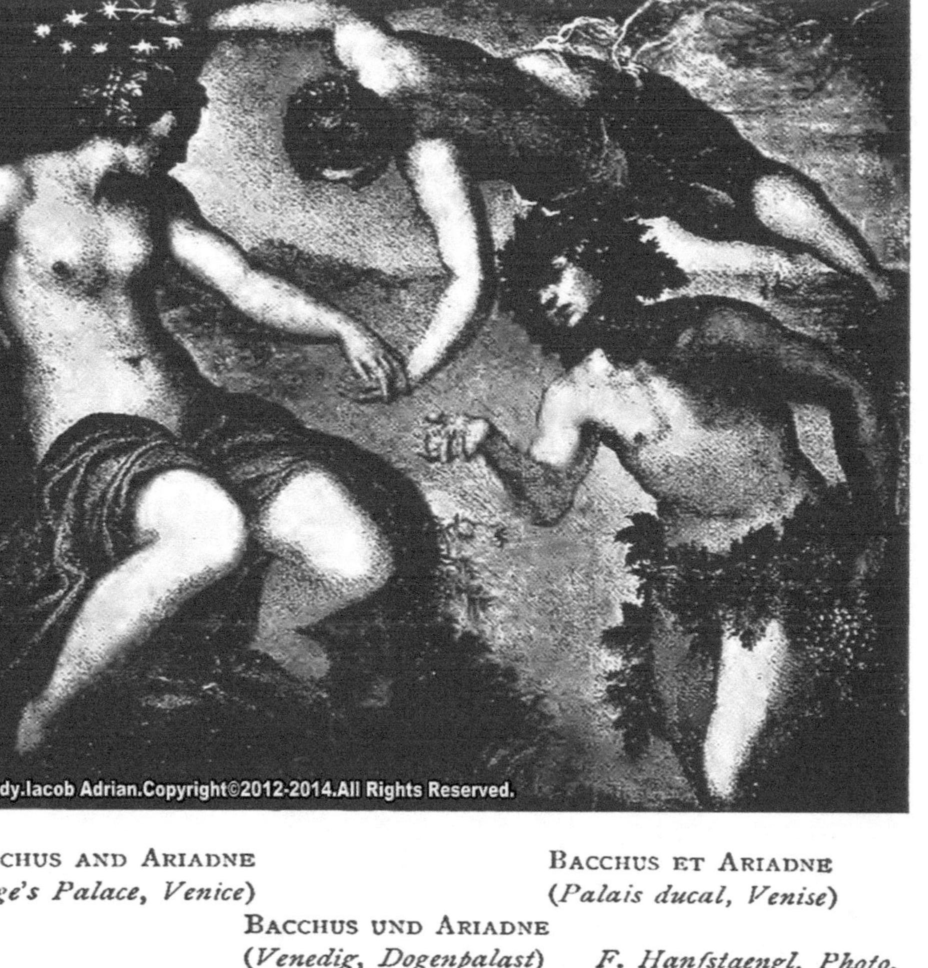

BACCHUS AND ARIADNE
(*Doge's Palace, Venice*)

BACCHUS ET ARIADNE
(*Palais ducal, Venise*)

BACCHUS UND ARIADNE
(*Venedig, Dogenpalast*)

F. Hanfstaengl, Photo.

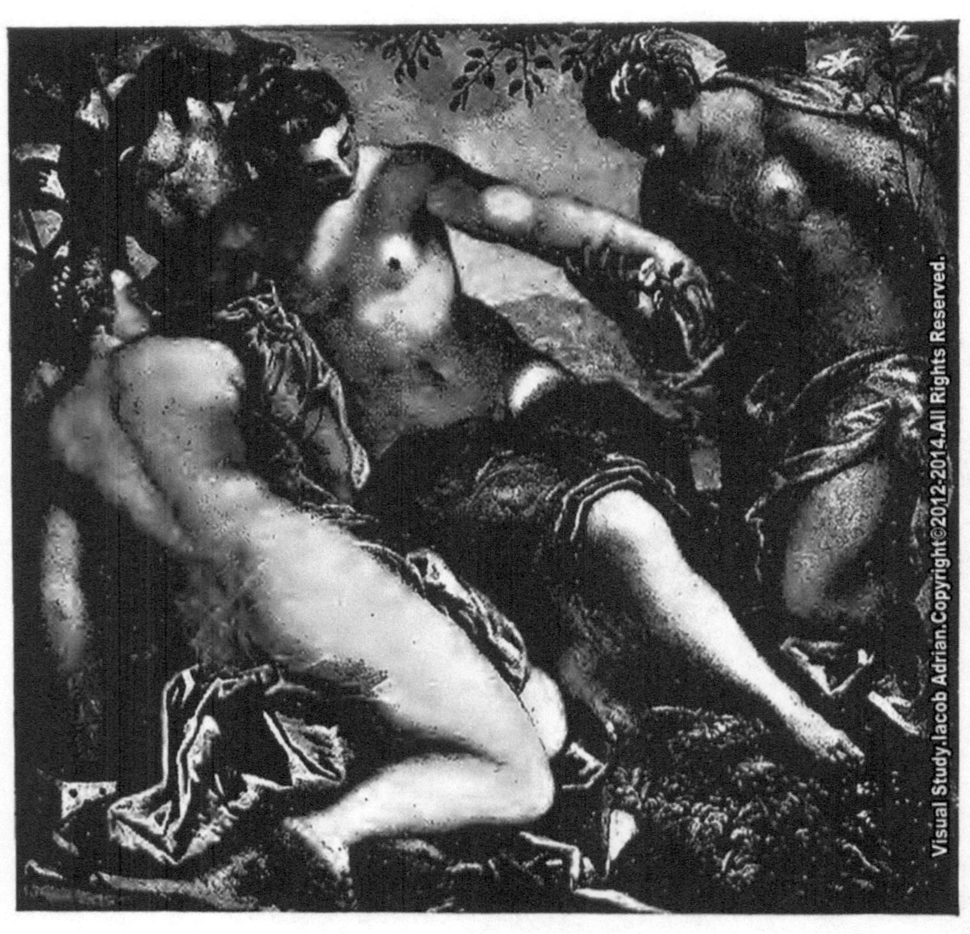

MERCURY AND THE GRACES
(*Doge's Palace, Venice*)

MERCURE ET LES GRÂCES
(*Palais ducal, Venise*)

MERKUR UND DIE GRAZIEN
(*Venedig, Dogenpalast*)

F. Hanfstaengl, Photo.

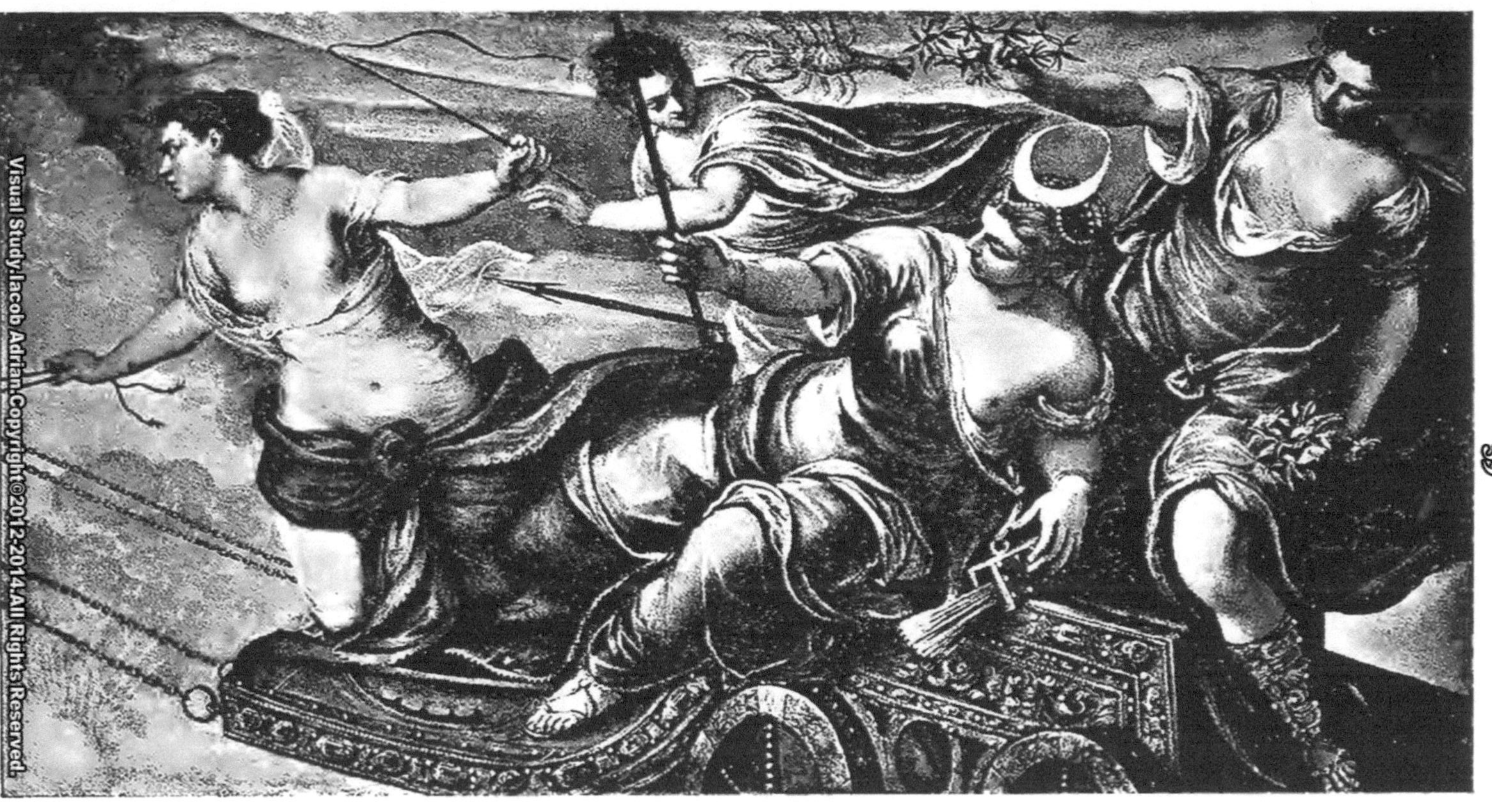

Luna with the Hours
(*Royal Gallery, Berlin*)

Luna mit den Horen
(*Berlin, Kgl. Galerie*)
F. Hanfstaengl, Photo.

Luna avec les Heures
(*Galerie royale, Berlin*)

Bibliographic sources :

The masterpieces of Tintoretto (1518-1594) Sixty reproductions of photographs from the original paintings, affording examples of the different characteristics of the artist's work (1908)

Author: Tintoretto, 1518-1594

Publisher: London [etc.] Gowan & Gray, ltd.

This documentary study use,
combined in various proportions,
elements from the following categories,
forms and subsets :
- fair use
- documentary
- documentary photography
- feature
- journalism
- arts journalism
- visual journalism
- photojournalism
- celebrity photography

in order to :
- employ material as the object of cultural critique ,
- quote to illustrate an argument or point ,
- use material in historical sequence,

providing independent opinion,
using photos, press articles, advertisements,
opinions of fans etc. ...

www.ingramcontent.com/pod-product-compliance
Lightning Source LLC
Chambersburg PA
CBHW021022180526
45163CB00005B/2074